THE HOLT GUIDE TO DOCUMENTATION AND WRITING IN THE DISCIPLINES

SECOND EDITION

KIRSZNER & MANDELL

Contributor

Feroza Jussawalla

University of Texas at El Paso

Holt, Rinehart and Winston, Inc.

Fort Worth   Chicago   San Francisco   Philadelphia
Montreal   Toronto   London   Sydney   Tokyo

CREDITS

"Mark Twain: Civil War Deserter?" reprinted from The *Rinehart Handbook for Writers* by Bonnie Carter and Craig Skates. Copyright © 1988 by Holt, Rinehart and Winston, Inc.

"The Study of Fossil Flowers" reprinted from *Writing Research Papers Across the Curriculum*, 2nd ed. by Susan Hubbuch. Copyright © 1989 by Holt, Rinehart and Winston, Inc.

"Civilian Control of Atomic Energy: Scientists' Bridge into Politics" reprinted from *Writing: a College Rhetoric*, 2nd ed. by Laurie Kirszner and Stephen Mandell. Copyright © 1988 by Holt, Rinehart and Winston, Inc.

ISBN 0-03-027927-5

Note: Parts of this work are derived from THE HOLT HANDBOOK, Second Edition by Laurie Kirszner and Stephen Mandell, Copyright © 1989, 1986 by Holt, Rinehart and Winston, Inc.

Printed in the United States of America

9 0 1 2   016   9 8 7 6 5 4 3 2 1

Holt, Rinehart and Winston, Inc.
The Dryden Press
Saunders College Publishing

ACKNOWLEDGMENTS

I am indebted to the librarians at the University of Texas—El Paso, biology professors Joann Ellzey and Lillian Mayberry, and history professor Tom Howard at Virginia Polytechnic Institute in Blacksburg, Virginia for their valuable assistance in the preparation of my contribution to this guide. I also thank my students, who let me reproduce their written assignments and the Ford Foundation grant for advanced literacy, which enabled me to develop several of the assignments.

El Paso, TX   Feroza Jussawalla
January, 1989

CONTENTS

THE HOLT GUIDE
TO DOCUMENTATION
AND WRITING
IN THE DISCIPLINES

TAKING NOTES:
SOME GENERAL ADVICE

After you have selected useful sources for your paper you are ready to begin your concentrated reading and note taking, focusing only on those sections of a work that pertain to your topic. Before you begin reading any book or article, survey it, checking the headings and subheadings in the table of contents, and especially the index, for subjects you need to read carefully or to skim. As you read, underline and annotate sources whenever possible; then take notes on index cards. Concentrated reading helps you narrow your focus still further as you see connections among ideas and develop new perspectives on your topic. As you read and take notes, you will move toward a thesis. Later, you will use these notes to help you plan and write your paper.

Note-taking skills are essential in academic writing. Once you have mastered these skills, you can apply them to writing assignments in any discipline.

MAKING NOTE CARDS

Using index cards may seem cumbersome, but their advantages become obvious when you go about arranging and rearranging material. Often you do not know where you will use a particular piece of information or whether you will use it at all. You will be constantly rearranging ideas, and the flexibility of index cards makes adding and deleting information and experimenting with different sequences possible. Students who take notes in a notebook or on a tablet find that they spend as much time untangling their notes as they do writing their paper.

At the top of each card, *include a short heading* that relates the information on your card to your topic. Later, this heading will help you make your outline.

Each card should *accurately identify the source* of the information you are recording. You need not include the complete citation, but you must include enough information to identify your source. "Wilson 72," for example, would send you back to your bibliography card carrying the complete documentation for *Patriotic Gore* by Edmund Wilson. For a book with more than one author, or for two books by the same author, you need a more complete reference. "Glazer & Moynihan 132," would suffice for *Beyond the Melting Pot* by Nathan Glazer and Daniel Patrick Moynihan. "Terkel, *Working* 135" would be necessary if you were using more than one book by Studs Terkel.

Here is one good note-card format.

```
                                    Art Style & Self Image          Short
                                                                    heading

Author,
page            Alschuler 260


Note              Children's view of themselves in society is
             reflected by their art style. A cramped, crowded
             art style using only a portion of the paper shows
             their limited role. The society consists of home,
             school, and friends.
```

As you take notes on note cards, you can do several things that will make the actual writing of your paper easier.

Put only one note on each card. If one card contains several different points, you will not be able to try out different ways of arranging those points.

Include everything now that you will need later to understand your note. You might think, for instance, that this makes sense:

Peyser—four important categories of new music

But in several weeks you will not remember what those four categories were. They should have been listed on your card.

Put an author's comments into your own words whenever possible. Word-for-word copying of information is probably the most inefficient way to take notes. Occasionally you will want to copy down a particularly memorable statement or the exact words of an expert on your topic, and such quotations can strengthen your paper. But in your final paper, for the most part, you will summarize and paraphrase your source material, adding your own observations and judgments. Putting information into your own words now keeps you from relying too heavily on the words of others or producing a paper that is a string of quotations rather than a thoughtful interpretation and analysis of ideas.

Remember to record your own observations and reactions. As you read your sources, get into the habit of writing down all the ideas—comments, questions, links with other sources, apparent contradictions, and so on—that occur to you. If you do not, you will probably forget them. But be sure to bracket your own reactions and observations so you will not confuse them with the author's material.

Indicate what kind of information is on your note card. If you copy an author's exact words, place them in quotation marks. If you use an author's ideas but not the exact words, do not use quotation marks. (Do not forget, however, to identify your source.) Finally, if you write down your own ideas, enclose them in brackets ([ ]). This system helps you avoid confusion—and plagiarism.

The student who wrote this note card was exploring the way the press portrayed President Richard Nixon during the Watergate crisis. Note that he has included only one note on his card, that both his note and its source are as complete as possible, and that he has clearly identified the first sentence as a summary ("The authors say . . .") and the other comments as his own.

                                                    Watergate
Bernstein & Woodward 366

    The authors say that by the summer of 1973
both Alexander Haig and Henry Kissinger urged
Richard Nixon to cut his ties with his aides. [Is
there any evidence of this? What sources support
this? Seems doubtful.]

QUOTATION NOTE CARD

You *quote* when you copy an author's remarks just as they appear in your source, word for word, including all punctuation, capitalization, and spelling. When recording quotations, enclose all words that are not your own within quotation marks and identify your source with appropriate documentation. Check carefully to make sure that you have not inadvertently left out quotation marks or miscopied material from your source.

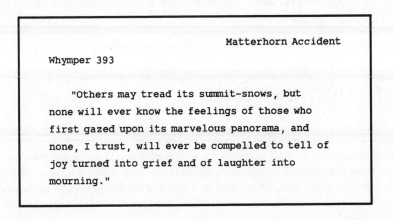

                                        Matterhorn Accident
Whymper 393

    "Others may tread its summit-snows, but
none will ever know the feelings of those who
first gazed upon its marvelous panorama, and
none, I trust, will ever be compelled to tell of
joy turned into grief and of laughter into
mourning."

PARAPHRASE NOTE CARD

A *paraphrase* is a detailed restatement, in your own words, of the *content* of a passage. In it you not only present the main points of your source, but retain their order and emphasis as well. A paraphrase will often include brief phrases quoted from the original to convey its tone or viewpoint. When you write a paraphrase, you should present only the author's ideas and keep your own interpretations, conclusions, and evaluations separate.

You paraphrase when you need detailed information from specific passages of a source but not the author's exact language. For this reason paraphrase is especially useful when you are presenting technical material to a general audience. It can also be helpful for reporting complex material or a particularly intricate discussion in easily understood terms. Although the author's concepts may be essential, the terms in which they are described could be far too difficult for your readers to follow. In such cases paraphrase enables you to give a complete sense of the author's ideas without using his or her words. Paraphrase is also useful when you want to convey the sense of a section of a work of literature or a segment of dialogue.

Original: Tyndall, <u>Hours of Exercise</u> (on the advantage of using a rope while mountain climbing):

> Not to speak of the moral effect of its presence, an amount of help upon a dangerous slope that might be measured by the gravity of a few pounds is often of incalculable importance.

```
                                                     Ropes
     Tyndall 289

          Aside from its psychological effect, a rope
     can be extremely important when a slight steadying
     pressure is necessary.
```

SUMMARY NOTE CARD

Unlike a paraphrase, which is a detailed restatement of a source, a *summary* is a general restatement, in your own words, of the *meaning* of a passage. Always much shorter than the original, a summary provides an overview of a piece of writing, focusing on the main idea. Because of its brevity, a summary usually eliminates the illustrations, secondary details, and asides that characterize the original. Like a paraphrase, a summary contains only the essence of a passage, not your interpretations or conclusions.

You summarize when you want to convey a general sense of an author's ideas to your readers. Summary is a useful technique when you want to record the main idea, but not the specific points or the exact words, of something that you have read. Because it need not follow the order or emphasis of a source, summary enables you to relate an author's ideas to your topic in a way that paraphrase and quotation do not.

```
                                            Ropes

     Tyndall 289-90

        In the 1800's, climbers thought ropes would
     help prevent falls by steadying mountain climbers
     who had lost their balance. However, the rope
     could be fatal to all tied to it if a climber
     actually fell.
```

COMPUTER NOTE TAKING

More and more researchers are beginning to save their notes on computer files. Sometimes this is done in the course of preparing an annotated bibliography. This task simplifies the preparation of your final paper greatly as it is often possible to copy sections from your notes into the main body of your paper. When you enter your notes into a "notes file" on computer, try to visualize your screen as an index card. Be sure to enter the complete bibliographic citation in the proper format. If you do so, you can assemble all the citations from your notes to prepare the bibliography.

EXERCISES

1. In the government-publication section of the library you find a book called *The Navajo Nation: An American Colony* which the United States Commission on Civil Rights published in Washington, D.C., in 1975. Its library call number is CR 1.2:N22/2. As you write a paper on the Navajo school systems which the government operates, you find this paragraph (pages 126–127):

Navajos, in fact, have been excluded from the decision-making process in these school systems. The result has been a variety of educational policies unrelated to the Navajo community. The Navajo language and culture have been largely ignored in the curriculum offered to Navajo students. Although an occasional course in the Navajo language is offered, there is little push to develop bilingual education and some schools still reprimand students and teachers for speaking Navajo. Nor has bicultural education had much support from non-Indian educational planners on the reservation. Insensitivity to Navajo culture is revealed dramatically in the preservation by many schools of a dress code requiring male students to keep their hair short, effectively preventing them from wearing the traditional "Navajo knot."

a. Prepare a note card quoting directly from the paragraph.

b. Prepare a three-line summary of the entire passage; use your own words.

c. Paraphrase the lines you quoted in Exercise 1a.

2. Use this passage from *Walden* by Henry David Thoreau for items a–c below.

No man ever stood the lower in my estimation for having a patch in his clothes; yet I am sure that there is greater anxiety, commonly, to have fashionable, or at least clean and unpatched clothes, than to have a sound conscience. But even if the rent is not mended, perhaps the worst vice betrayed is improvidence. I sometimes try my acquaintances by such tests as this: Who could wear a patch, or two extra seams only, over the knee? Most behave as if they believed that their prospects for life would be ruined if they should do it. It would be easier for them to hobble to town with a broken leg than with a broken pantaloon.

a. Make a quotation note card using the last sentence from the selection above.

b. Make a paraphrase using the same sentence.

c. Make a brief summary card using the entire passage. You don't need to capture every idea—just what you consider important.

3. Here is another passage from *Walden*. Use it to answer items a and b below.

But men labor under a mistake. The better part of the man is soon plowed into the soil for compost. By a seeming fate, commonly called necessity, they are employed, as it says in an old book, laying up treasures which moth and rust will corrupt and thieves break through and steal. It is a fool's life, as they will find when they get to the end of it, if not before.

a. Make a quotation note card using the second sentence.

b. Make a brief summary card for the entire passage. Again, you do not need to capture every idea—just what you consider important.

Exercises adapted from *The Practical Writer*, 3rd ed. by Edward Bailey, Philip Powell, and Jack Shuttleworth, (New York: Holt, Rinehart and Winston, 1986).

ACADEMIC WRITING

FOCUSING ON A MAIN IDEA

The most important common factor in writing college papers in all the different subject areas is the need to focus on a main idea and to support that main idea with findings from your research. As you go through your notes, try to see if there is one single idea that occurs over and over again or one single point around which different ideas come together. Such a central focus should become the main idea of your paper. It is important as you choose what the main idea of your paper will be that you keep in mind whether it interests you or not and what you know about it. Your *interest* and *knowledge of the subject matter* should help to determine the central focus of your paper. The central focus of your paper, or your main idea, should be expressed in a single sentence at the beginning of your paper, preferably after your introduction. Topic sentences of subsequent sections should relate to that main idea.

SUPPORTING A MAIN IDEA WITH RESEARCH

All of the major subject areas you study in college require you to support your main idea with research, either the ideas of others that you have gathered from interviews or your research sources or original data that you have collected. Although library research is sometimes sufficient, particularly in the humanities, other subject areas often use methods of data collection like field research, case studies, analyses of statistics, and questionnaires.

Once you have located your sources, you must read and think critically about your material. Ask yourself how relevant, valid, and accurate your sources are. If your sources are not believable, your readers will question your credibility as a researcher and the point of view you develop in your thesis. Therefore, as you choose the research materials to support your thesis—and later, as you read and take notes—you need to make judgments about your sources.

ORGANIZING IDEAS

Once you have a main idea for your paper, you need to organize your information into smaller categories, each of which should be unified by a topic sentence that relates to the thesis and expresses a related idea. Each topic sentence will be supported by specific details and examples culled from your research. For instance, a sociological description of the "working mother" might provide these particulars: aged 34, 81.6% employed with a household income of $40,500, interested in buying self-improvement, career guidance, jewelry and beauty aids. Such facts and figures that you collected in an interview can help to support a general point you might wish to make about the working mother.

Papers in all academic disciplines often include the following components.

1. An introduction in which you identify a focused topic and present your point of view, the thesis of the paper.
2. A short literature survey of other points of view on your topic—that is, background on the topic. This summary could be a narrative paragraph that shows how the research is pertinent to your thesis.
3. Evidence to support your thesis.
4. Acknowledgment of opposing points of view and their differences from your point of view.
5. A conclusion that restates your thesis.

This general arrangement covers a wide array of papers. Suppose, for instance, you were arguing the benefits to children of having a working mother. After using an interesting anecdote or example or statistic that had appeared in a newspaper, you could state the following specific thesis: "Children of working mothers often develop better social skills and greater financial responsibility as a result of their experiences in child care." This thesis could be followed by a narrative paragraph describing the available information on the development of children of working mothers. You would then go on to break down the thesis into its major parts. After supporting each aspect of your thesis with evidence, you can present opposing points of view and show their shortcomings. Then, restate your thesis in your conclusion. This general arrangement is appropriate for papers in all academic disciplines.

More specifically, all academic disciplines rely on certain familiar patterns of organizing material. *Comparison and contrast* is one such standard method of arranging ideas. In comparison and contrast you bring together the similarities and dissimilarities of the subjects you are writing about by focusing on a particular topic idea. Here, for instance, is a paragraph from a sociology textbook.

Clearly Mexican-Americans have faced a great deal of prejudice and discrimination. Like blacks, Mexican-Americans were segregated in restaurants, housing, schools, public facilities, and so on. They were frequently the victims of violence, which included beatings by police and servicemen. Today, the effects of the prejudice and discrimination directed against Mexican-Americans can still be seen. For instance, they are more likely than Anglos to hold blue-collar jobs with a large number in service jobs such as janitors. Their unemployment rate averages about 6 points more than that for Anglos. Their median family income is only about 74 percent of the income of Anglo families. Mexican-Americans are more likely than both blacks and Anglos to experience job layoffs and cutbacks in work time. About 36 percent of the teenagers drop out of school, which is more than twice the rate for Anglo teenagers and almost double the rate for black teenagers (from Daniel J. Curran and Claire H. Renzetti, *Social Problems: Society in Crisis*, Boston: Allyn and Bacon, 1987).

Often information is organized in the order in which it occurs or in the order in which a procedure is carried out. For instance, a history paper might be organized *chronologically*, following the order in which certain historical battles were fought; a section of a scientific paper might be organized as a *process*, following the step-by-step procedure of a scientific experiment or describing a natural process such as digestion. Other familiar patterns of organizing ideas include *cause and effect* and *classification*.

ASSIGNMENTS IN ACADEMIC WRITING

All academic disciplines share certain assignments. For instance, in any discipline you may be required to write a literature survey, an abstract, or a proposal. In addition, each discipline has certain assignments—laboratory reports and case studies, for example—that are not particular to it.

The most common assignments in college writing ask you to analyze a problem, a situation, or a work such as a literary text. The result is analytic papers in which you research a specific problem, gather data related to that problem, and propose specific solutions or applications of your solutions. These assignments usually require original thought, a clear statement of the problem, and suggested solutions. Most academic papers require research whether it is done in the library or the laboratory. Here is a research assignment from a marketing class.

Provide your classmates with a list of subsidiaries owned by a parent corporation. Example: General Electric owns RCA, RCA owns Avis Car Rentals and Random House Publishers, Random House owns Harlequin, and so on. Take a survey about the major companies with which your fellow students have had negative or positive experiences, including the number of times they have dealt with a company and what the results of their dealings have been. Can you make any generalizations about major conglomerates and their subsidiaries and how they affect the ordinary consumer? Should Congress pass laws that restrict the size of the companies? Write a research paper for your congressional representative explaining why he or she should support or reject such legislation.

Here is an English assignment that requires you to research dialects of English.

> Write or tell a story about the area in which you grew up. Analyze your story to see whether you have used localized idiomatic phrases. Do your classmates understand them? Are there phrases they have used that you cannot understand? Can you define the particular dialect you are using? After doing some library research, write a paper for an audience of foreign students about how English usage varies across the United States.

Other assignments may require you to gather information about an area and its culture. For instance, in history you may be asked to gather the story of the Tigua Indians; in political science you may be asked to talk to county officers or other local politicians. In these cases you will report on your findings. Writing a coherent report requires focusing on a single idea and gathering specifics and details.

RESEARCH RESOURCES

The reference section of any library is the best place to find general research sources. The reference section of the library contains sources as diverse as encyclopedias, atlases, quotation books, and bibliographies as well as information which indicates where you actually find other material. In addition to the card catalog of the library, the reference section contains indexes, bibliographies, and computerized materials that can tell you where to find material on the research topic of your choice. One way to start your research is to browse in the subject section of your card catalog. If you cannot find your topic in the subject section, search *The Library of Congress Subject Headings*, which usually list the various names under which a subject might be listed.

General Library Sources

The following list is a guide to some of the major sources—indexes, encyclopedias, bibliographies, and other library materials—that you can use to find general research information.

Indexes
Biography Index
Government Documents Index

Magazine Index
New York Times Index
Public Affairs Information Services Index
Reader's Guide to Periodical Literature
Wall Street Journal Index
Washington Post Index

Encyclopedias
Academic American Encyclopedia
Encyclopedia Americana
Encyclopaedia Britannica
Micropaedia
Propaedia
The New Columbia Encyclopedia
The Random House Encyclopedia

Bibliographies
Books in Print
The Bibliographic Index
The Subject Guide to Books in Print
Paperbound Books in Print

Other Sources
Dissertation Abstracts International
Editorials on File
Monthly Catalog of United States Government Publications
Historical Atlas
Encyclopedia Britannica World Atlas
Facts on File
Statistical Abstracts
World Almanac

General Databases for Computer Searches

In many cases computerized searching makes research much faster and provides the option of combining subject concepts (key words) with author and title information to find exact citations. For instance, you may know only that Fredric Jameson has written an article on Third World literature, but not where it has been published or the exact title or contents. Since the article is about literature, you decide to search a literature database such as a Bibliography, or the MLA, which yields various titles by Fredric Jameson. Matching the titles found with the subject "Third World Literature," you find the following: Jameson, Fredric, "World Literature in an Age of Multinational Capitalism," in *The Current in Criticism* edited by Clayton Koelb and Virgil Lokke.

Some of the most widely used general databases include the *Magazine Index*, *Dissertation Abstracts Online*, *Biography Index*, *Books in Print*, *GPO Monthly Catalog*, *Newsearch*, *National Newspaper Index*, *New York Times Index*, *Marquis Who's Who*, and the *Readers' Guide to Periodical Literature*.

It is important to remember that although many databases have a print counterpart, some are available only on-line.

CD-ROM is a rapidly expanding new technology for database searching which is available in many libraries. Many indexes that are available in a print version are now offered on CD-ROM. CD-ROM offers a cost savings over on-line database searching and more flexibility than searching print indexes.

DOCUMENTING SOURCES

Documentation is the acknowledgment of what you have derived from a source and of exactly where in that source you found your material. Not all fields use the same style of documentation. The most widely used formats are those advocated by the Modern Language Association (MLA), and the American Psychological Association (APA). In addition, the sciences, engineering, and medicine have their own formats. Before writing a paper in any of these areas, you should ask your instructor what style of documentation you should use and then follow it consistently throughout your paper (see Overview of Documentation Styles, p. 145).

What to Document

You must document all materials that you borrow from your sources. Documentation enables your readers to identify your sources and to judge the quality of your work. It also encourages them to look up the books and articles that you cite. Therefore, you should carefully document the following kinds of information:

1. direct quotations
2. summaries or paraphrases of material from your sources
3. opinions, judgments, and original insights of others
4. illustrations, tables, graphs, and charts that you get from your sources

The references in your text should clearly point a reader to the borrowed material and should clearly differentiate your ideas from the ideas of your sources.

What Not to Document

Common knowledge, information that you would expect most educated readers to know, need not be documented. You can assume, for instance, that undocumented information that appears in several of your sources is generally known. You can also safely include facts that are widely used in encyclopedias, textbooks, newspapers, and magazines, or on television and radio. Even if the information is new to you, as long as it is generally accepted as fact, you need not indicate your source. However, information that is in dispute or that is credited to a particular person, should be documented. You need not, for example, document the fact that the Declaration of Independence was signed on July 4, 1776, or that Josiah Bartlett and Oliver Wolcott signed it. However, you do have to document a historian's analysis of the document, or a particular scholar's recent discoveries about Josiah Bartlett.

As you can see, when to document is sometimes a matter of judgment. As a beginning researcher, you should document any material you believe might need acknowledgment, even if you suspect it might be common knowledge. By doing so, you avoid the possibility of plagiarism.

SUMMARY

In general, then, in all the papers you will be asked to write in college you will be required to express a central idea clearly and to ensure that the researched material relates to the thesis and is organized in clearly identifiable patterns. However, each of the three broad disciplinary areas—the humanities, the social sciences, and the sciences—has its own particular research sources, paper formats, assignments, styles, and methods of documentation. The sections that follow discuss the differences in the three disciplinary areas.

WRITING IN THE HUMANITIES

The humanities include a variety of subjects, including art, music, literature, history, languages, and philosophy. Some of these disciplines use different documentation styles and special library sources.

RESEARCH SOURCES

Library research is an important part of study in many humanities disciplines. When you begin your research in any subject area, the *Humanities Index* is one general source you can turn to. There are also many specialized sources available as you continue your research process.

Specialized Library Sources

The following list represents some of the sources used often in the various humanities disciplines.

Art
Art Index
Art Reproductions in Books
McGraw-Hill Encyclopedia of World Art
New Dictionary of Modern Sculpture
Oxford Companion to Art

Drama
New York Times Theatre Reviews
McGraw-Hill Encyclopedia of World Drama
Modern World Drama: An Encyclopedia
Oxford Companion to the Theatre

Film
Guide to Critical Reviews
International Index to Multimedia Information
Lander's Film Reviews
New York Times Film Reviews

History
Cambridge Ancient History
Cambridge Medieval History
CRIS (Combined Retrospective Index to Journals in History, 1838–1974)

Great Events in History
Guide to Historical Literature
Harvard Guide to American History
Historical Abstracts (Europe)
New Cambridge Modern History

Language and Literature
Annual Bibliography of English Language and Literature
Biography Index
Book Review Digest
Book Review Index
Children's Literature Abstracts
Contemporary Authors
Current Biography
Essay and General Literature Index
LHUS (Literary History of the United States)
LLBA (Language and Language Behavior Abstracts)
MLA International Bibliography
Oxford Companion to American Literature
Oxford Companion to Classical Literature
Oxford Companion to English Literature
Princeton Encyclopedia of Poetry and Poetics
PMLA General Index, v. 1–50
Salem Press' Critical Surveys of Poetry, Fiction, Long Fiction, and Drama
Short Story Index
Webster's Biographical Dictionary
Twentieth Century Authors

Music
Grove's Dictionary of Music and Musicians
Harvard Dictionary of Music
Music Article Guide
Music Index

Philosophy
The Concise Encyclopedia of Western Philosophy and Philosophers
Encyclopedia of Philosophy
Philosopher's Index

Specialized Databases for Computer Searches

Many of the print indexes that appear on the above list of specialized library sources are also available on-line. Some of the most helpful databases for humanities disciplines include *Humanities Index, Art Index, MLA Bibliography, Religion Index, Philosopher's Index, RILM Abstracts, Essay and General Literature Index, Artbibliographies Modern, Historical Abstracts,* the *LLBA Index,* and *Comprehensive Dissertation Abstracts.*

Non-Library Sources

Research in the humanities is not always limited to the library. Historians may need to do oral interviews or archival work or consult papers collected in town halls, churches, or court houses. Art majors may need to visit museums and galleries. Attending concerts is a legitimate form of field work for music majors.

Non-library sources can be important additions to a paper in any humanities discipline. For instance, in writing about history you not only study the events of the past, but you also interpret the information that you collect. It is then up to you to defend your interpretation of those events. The following excerpt from a student's oral history interview was a valuable resource for her paper about Tigua Indians.

> Arturo Tapia, a registered Tigua Indian, recalls, "My daddy never used to say he was Tigua Indian . . . we never talked about it . . . other Indians never liked us and the white people never allowed us in their bars or stores. I have gone up to people and told them I am Tigua and they say, "What a low class Indian,' or "Them down there, the Mexicans,' 'They sold out.'

The student who recorded this interview chose to use it in her opening paragraph, to help introduce her paper's thesis.

> The history of the Tiguas is full of misconceptions. The New Mexico version of the Tiguas' migration is that they fled with a Spanish party to El Paso during the Indian uprising of August 10, 1680, while the Tigua version of their migration is quite different. The New Mexico Indians have portrayed the Tiguas of Isleta as a "Judas Tribe" who turned against their own people to ally with the Spanish. Even today the Tiguas face discrimination from other Indians as well as from whites and feel they are considered "low class" (Rosario).

ASSIGNMENTS IN THE HUMANITIES

The Reaction Paper

One assignment particular to the humanities is the reaction paper, in which you analyze and interpret your responses to a work. In such a paper you are simply asked to express your personal reaction to a work such as Keats's "Ode to a Grecian Urn" or to a painting or to a concert you attended. Such an assignment requires you to write a first-person account of your feelings upon encountering a work and to account, if you can, for what influenced your response.

The Book Review

A book review summarizes or outlines a book and provides your evaluation of it. Book reviews are assigned in all the humanities disciplines, particularly literature, history, and philosophy, and in most cross-disciplinary humanities or general education sequences. Here is a sample book review from *World Literature Today*, Spring 1988.

> Timothy Mo's novel *An Insular Possession* is a rather slow-moving account of British colonizers in the Far East. . . . Walter Eastman, one of the principal characters, calls himself, in a letter, a "philosopher of the verandah." Even the American characters are infected with British practices, as they are with loathing for their steamy surroundings and the natives.
>
> What Mo does do beautifully is evoke that languid, steamy existence. In his delicate and beautifully written descriptions he shows the power of the English language in the hands of non-native English-speaking ex-colonials. His characters O'Rourke and Eastman are painters, metaphors for the author himself as he paints with delicate strokes these lives lived under muslin nets and the East as seen out of these nets.

The Art Review

Art reviews are similar to book reviews in that they assess the worth of a work of art or of an artist. Here is an excerpt from "Tom Mulder: Painting Indians" in *Utah Holiday*, October 18, 1976.

> I stand before a picture in Phillips Art Gallery in Salt Lake City, Utah. Suddenly home (India) is vividly alive. It spreads beyond the canvas and encapsulates me. I can feel the rhythm of the movements, as three women carry brass pots on their heads and can hear the clinking of their anklets. With his view of both cultures, Southwestern American and subcontinental Asian, Mulder feels one could transport a subcontinental village to the American Southwest, take an Indian posture and make of it a Navajo. The American Southwest of these paintings feels curiously like home. The color, the light are essentially the same; and yet the rugweaver is a Navajo. An artist seeing similarities between two types of "Indians"?

The Bibliographic Essay

A bibliographic essay surveys research in the field and compares and contrasts the usefulness of various sources on a particular subject. Several publications in the humanities publish bibliographic essays on a yearly basis to inform scholars of the yearly developments in the field. Here, for example, is a short excerpt from the "Pound and Eliot" chapter of *American Literary Scholarship*.

> This has been a good year for theoretical work on Pound. Martin A. Kayman connects Pound's theory of the image to his theory of money in "Ezra Pound: The Color of His Money" (*Paideuma* 15, ii-iii: 39–52). I find Kayman's argument here interesting but problematic in his unexamined assumption that Pound never changed, that the aesthetics of 1912–14 are the same as the politics of the 1930s. That is explicitly the argument of an unintelligent essay by Robert Lumsden, "Ezra Pound's Imagism" (*Paideuma* 15, ii-iii: 253–64) who argues that Pound remained an imagist and that there is no significant distinction between image, vortex, ideoplasty and ideogram.

Note that in a bibliographic essay the author must include both his or her assessment of the work at hand and the full citation of the source. This differs from the annotated bibliography in which, in the annotation or the summary assessment, you try *not* to interject a personal point of view and do *not* include the author's name, the work's title, or publication information within the summary.

The Annotated Bibliography

Each entry in an annotated bibliography includes the full citation of a reference source and a short summary or abstract of the source. The abstract should be a distilled, factual summary; brevity is important. Try not to include any material from the citation in the text of the abstract. For example:

Stead, C.K. *Pound, Yeats, Eliot and the Modernist Movement*. New Brunswick: Rutgers University Press, 1986.

> Stead's overall theses are as follows: (1) Pound and Eliot are central modernists; Yeats is not; and (2) Pound's politics are less distasteful than Eliot's because Pound at least had the courage of his convictions. The value of the book lies in Stead's close readings of many poems by Pound, Eliot, and Yeats. This general thrust is to show Eliot's deep influence on Pound in matters of form and technique.

CONVENTIONS OF STYLE AND FORMAT

The humanities paper is a single unit in which all the paragraphs are connected to the thesis and to one another. Although papers may include internal headings and abstracts, they do not always do so. Writing in the humanities can be less formal than in the social sciences and sciences and may be directed at a lay audience. Note, for example, how much less formal the art review is than the other examples of common assignments. The book review is descriptive and evaluative while the bibliographic essay is more precise. Notice that the entry for the annotated bibliography is most concise and specific. Clarity and restraint from the overuse of jargon are important considerations. Writing in the first person is acceptable when you are expressing your own reactions and convictions. In other cases, however, you should use an objective tone and write in the third person [he, she, it].

In writing papers for literature, certain conventions of literary analysis are required. You may need to analyze the way a work is constructed. For example: Is it a novel that relies heavily on flashbacks? How does that structure affect the author's purpose or theme? As points of entry into literary analysis you can look at subjects like plot, characterization, theme, the use of imagery, and the writer's style. Literary analysis can be formal, historical, psychoanalytical, or economic. Keep in mind that it is not possible to concern yourself with all of these issues in one paper. You need to decide on one approach and one point of view and then develop that point of view in your paper.

DOCUMENTATION FORMATS

Like all other disciplines most of the subject areas in the humanities use documentation formats particular to the subject. English and modern and classical language scholars use the MLA format; art, history, music and philosophy scholars use *The Chicago Manual of Style*. Researchers in linguistics and languages use the *Handbook of the Linguistics Society of America* and sometimes the APA format used by the social sciences. (See page 74 for information on the APA style.)

THE MLA FORMAT*

The MLA format is recommended by the Modern Language Association of America, a professional organization of more than 25,000 teachers of English and other

*MLA documentation format follows the guidelines set in the *MLA Handbook for Writers of Research Papers*, 3rd ed. New York: MLA, 1988.

languages. It is required by teachers in the humanities at colleges throughout the United States and Canada. This method of documentation has three parts: parenthetical references in the text, a list of works cited, and explanatory notes. Full sample papers illustrating the MLA format begin on pages 41 and 53.

Parenthetical References in the Text

MLA documentation uses references inserted in parentheses within the text and keyed to a list of works cited at the end of the paper. A typical reference consists of the author's last name and a page number.

```
The colony's religious and political freedom appealed to
many idealists in Europe (Ripley 132).
```

If you use more than one source by the same author, shorten the title of each work to one or two key words and include the appropriate shortened title in the parenthetical reference.

```
Penn emphasized his religious motivation (Kelley, William
Penn 116).
```

If the author's name or the title of the work is stated in the text, do not include it in the parenthetical reference. Only a page reference is necessary.

```
Penn's political motivation is discussed by Joseph P.
Kelley in Pennsylvania, The Colonial Years, 1681-1776 (44).
```

Keep in mind that you punctuate differently with paraphrases and summaries, direct quotations run in with the text, and quotations that are set off from the text.

Parenthetical documentation for *paraphrases and summaries* should appear *before* terminal punctuation marks.

```
Penn's writings epitomize seventeenth-century religious
thought (Degler and Curtis 72).
```

Parenthetical documentation for *direct quotations run in with the text* should appear *after* the quotation marks but *before* the terminal punctuation.

```
As Ross says, "Penn followed his conscience in all matters"
(127).
```

```
We must now ask, as Ross does, "Did Penn follow Quaker
dictates in his dealings with the Indians" (128)?
```

```
According to Williams, "Penn's utopian vision was informed
by his Quaker beliefs . . ." (72).
```

Parenthetical documentation for *quotations that are set off from the text* should appear two spaces *after* the final punctuation.

```
. . . a commonwealth in which all individuals can
follow God's truth and develop according to God's
will. (Smith 314)
```

Sample References

Parenthetical references are a straightforward and easy way to provide documentation. Here are the forms required in some special situations.

Works by more than one author

```
One group of physicists questioned many of the assumptions
of relativity (Harbeck and Johnson 31).
```

```
With the advent of behaviorism psychology began a new phase
of inquiry (Cowen, Barbo, and Crum 31-34).
```

For books with more than three authors, list the first author followed by *et al.* ("and others") in place of the rest.

```
A number of important discoveries were made off the coast of
Crete in 1960 (Dugan et al. 63).
```

Two or more works by the same author

To cite two or more works by the same author, include the author's last name plus a comma; the complete title, if it is brief, or a shortened version; and the page reference. Thus two novels by Saul Bellow, Seize the Day and Henderson the Rain King, would be cited (Bellow, Seize the Day 53) and (Bellow, Henderson 89).

Works with a volume and page number

A colon separates volume and page numbers of books. The number before the colon is the volume number; the number after the colon is the page number.

> In 1912 Virginia Stephen married Leonard Woolf, with whom
> she founded the Hogarth Press (Woolf 1: 17).

Works without a listed author

For works without a listed author, use a shortened version of the title in the parenthetical reference.

> Television ratings wars have escalated during the past ten
> years ("Leaving the Cellar" 102).

Omit the page reference if you are citing a one-page article.

> It is a curious fact that the introduction of Christianity
> at the end of the Roman Empire "had no effect on the
> abolition of slavery" ("Slavery").

Indirect sources

Indicate that material is from an indirect source by using the abbreviation *qtd. in* ("quoted in") as part of the parenthetical reference.

> Wagner said that myth and history stood before him "with
> opposing claims" (qtd. in Winkler 10).

More than one work within a parenthesis

You may cite more than one work within a single parenthesis. Cite each work as you normally would, separating one from another with semicolons.

> The Brooklyn Bridge has been used as a subject by many
> American artists (McCullough 144; Tshjian 58).

Whenever possible, present long references as explanatory notes (see page 34).

Two authors with the same last name

When two of the authors you cite in your paper have the same last name, include the first names or initials in your references. For example, references in the same paper to Wilbert Snow's "The Robert Frost I Knew" and C.P. Snow's "The Two Cultures" would be (Wilbert Snow 37) and (C.P. Snow 71).

Literary works

In citations to prose works it is often helpful to include more than just author and page number. For example, the chapter number of a novel enables readers to locate your reference in any edition of the work to which you are referring. In parenthetical references to prose works, begin with the page number, include a semicolon, and add any additional information that might be necessary.

```
In Moby-Dick Melville refers to a whaling expedition funded
by Louis XIV of France (151; ch. 24).
```

In parenthetical references to poems, separate the divisions and line numbers with periods. Titles of books in the Bible are often abbreviated (Gen. 5.12). In the following citation the reference is to book 8, page 124 of The Aeneid.

```
Virgil describes the ships as cleaving the "green woods
reflected in the calm water" (The Aeneid 8.124).
```

An entire work

When citing an entire work rather than part of a work, all you need to do is include the author's last name in your text. If you wish, you may mention the author's name in a parenthetical reference.

```
Northrup Frye's Fearful Symmetry presents a complex
critical interpretation of Blake's poetry.
```

```
Fearful Symmetry presents a complex critical interpretation
of Blake's poetry (Frye).
```

Tables and illustrations

When citing tables and illustrations, include the documentation below the illustrative material.

```
Miscues which alter meaning            51%
Overall loss of comprehension          40%
Retelling score                        20%

Source: Alice S. Horning, "The Trouble with Writing Is the
Trouble with Reading," Journal of Basic Writing 6 (1987): 46.
```

The List of Works Cited

Your parenthetical references are keyed to a *Works Cited* section that lists all the books, articles, interviews, letters, films, and other sources that you use in your paper. If your instructor wants you to include all the sources you consulted, whether you actually cite them or not, use the title *Works Consulted*.

Arrangement of Citations

Your *Works Cited* section should begin on a new, numbered page after your last page of text. For example, if the text of your paper ends on page 7, then your works cited list will begin on page 8. The heading *Works Cited* should be centered one inch from the top of the paper. Skip two lines and begin each entry flush with the left-hand margin. Subsequent lines of the entry should be indented five spaces from the margin. Double space within and between entries.

In general, entries are arranged alphabetically, according to the last name of each author or to the first word of the title if the author is not known. Articles—*a, an,* and *the*—at the beginning of a title are not considered first words.

Capitalize the first words, last words, and all important words of the title. Do not capitalize articles, prepositions introducing phrases, coordinating conjunctions, and the *to* of infinitives (unless such words are the first or last words in the title). To conserve space, use a shortened form of the publisher's name, and do not include words such as *Incorporated, Company,* or *Publishers* after the name of the publisher. Thus *Holt, Rinehart and Winston* and *Oxford University Press, Inc.* become *Holt* and *Oxford UP.* When a publisher lists offices in several cities, give only the first; for cities outside the United States, add an abbreviation of the country if the city would be ambiguous or unfamiliar to readers (Birmingham, Eng., for example).

Sample Citations—Books

If you are citing books, your entries will contain this information:

1. The author's name (last name first) followed by a period and two spaces
2. The title, underlined and followed by a period and two spaces
3. The city of publication, followed by a colon
4. The shortened name of the publisher, followed by a comma
5. The year of publication, followed by a period

Notice that an entry has three main divisions separated from one another by two spaces and a period:

author (last name first)   *title*   *publication information*
          ↓   ↓   ↓
Barsan, Richard Meran. Non-Fiction Film. New York: Dutton, 1973.

The following examples illustrate some special situations in which you must vary this basic format.

A book by one author

Zagorin, Perez. The Court and the Country: The Beginning of the
    English Revolution. New York: Atheneum, 1970.

When citing an edition other than the first, indicate the edition number in the form used on the work's title page.

Lawrence, William W. Shakespeare's Problem Comedies. 2nd ed. New
    York: Ungar, 1960.

If the book you are citing contains a title enclosed in quotation marks, keep the quotation marks. If the book contains an underlined title, however, do not underline it in your citation.

Herzog, Alan, ed. Twentieth Century Interpretations of "To a
    Skylark." Englewood Cliffs: Prentice, 1975.

A book by two or three authors

Only the first author's name is entered in reverse order; names of the second and third authors appear in normal order. Enter the names in the order in which they appear on the title page. State each name in full even if two authors have the same last name.

> Feldman, Burton, and Robert D. Richardson. <u>The Rise of Modern</u>
> <u>Mythology</u>. Bloomington: Indiana UP, 1972.

A book by more than three authors

For books with more than three authors, list the first author followed by *et al.* (and others).

> Prinz, Martin, et al., eds. <u>Guide to Rocks and Minerals</u>. New York:
> Simon, 1978.

Two or more books by the same author

When listing two books by the same author, include the name in the first entry, but substitute three hyphens followed by a period in subsequent entries. Entries should be arranged alphabetically according to title.

> Kingston, Maxine Hong. <u>China Men</u>. New York: Knopf, 1980.
> ---. <u>The Woman Warrior</u>. New York: Vintage, 1977.

A multivolume work

If you use one volume of a multiple volume work, give the volume number and the total number of volumes, even if your paper refers to only one volume.

> Brown, T. Allston. Vol. 2 of <u>A History of the New York Stage</u>. 3 vols.
> New York: Blom, 1903.

A multivolume work in which each volume has an individual title

> Durant, Will. <u>The Renaissance</u>. Vol. 5 of <u>The Story of Civilization</u>.
> 11 vols. New York: Simon, 1953.

An edited book

When listing an edited book, begin with the author if you refer mainly to the text itself.

> Melville, Herman. Moby Dick. Ed. Charles Fiedelson, Jr.
> Indianapolis: Bobbs, 1964.

If the citations in your paper are to the work of the editor—the introduction, the editor's notes, or the editor's decisions in editing the text—put his or her name before the title.

> Edel, Leon, ed. The Future of the Novel: Essays on the Art of Fiction.
> By Henry James. New York: Vintage, 1956.

An essay appearing in an anthology

When your paper refers to a single essay in a collection of essays, cite the single essay, not the collection. List the author of the essay first, and include all the pages on which the full essay appears, even if you cite only one page in your paper.

> Forster, E. M. "Flat and Round Characters." Theory of the Novel. Ed.
> Philip Stevick. New York: Free, 1980. 223-231.

If the essay you cite has been published previously, include publishing data for the first publication followed by the current information along with the abbreviation *Rpt. in* (Reprinted in).

> Ong, Walter J. "Literacy and Orality in Our Times." ADE Bulletin 58
> (1978): 1-7. Rpt. in Composition and Literature: Bridging the
> Gap. Ed. Winifred Bryan Horner. Chicago: U of Chicago P, 1983.
> 126-140.

A cross-reference

If you use more than one essay from a collection, list each essay, separately, including a cross reference to the collection. In addition, list complete publication information for the collection itself.

```
Bolgar, R. R.  "The Greek Legacy."  Finley 429-72.
Davies, A. M.  "Lyric and Other Poetry."  Finley 93-119.
Finley, M. I., ed.  The Legacy of Greece.  New York: Oxford UP, 1981.
```

An introduction, preface, foreword, or afterword of a book

```
Beauvoir, Simone de.  Preface.  Treblinka.  By Jean-Francois Steiner.
    New York: Mentor, 1979.  xiii-xxii.
```

A translation

```
Carpentier, Alejo.  Reasons of State.  Trans. Francis Partridge.  New
    York: Norton, 1976.
```

An unsigned article in an encyclopedia

List an unsigned article the way it is cited in the encyclopedia. Because encyclopedia articles are arranged alphabetically, you may omit the volume and page numbers when citing one. You do not have to include publication information for well known reference books.

```
"Liberty, Statue of."  Encyclopaedia Britannica: Macropaedia.
    1985 ed.
```

A signed article in an encyclopedia

Cite a signed article by stating the author's last name first, followed by the article's title. When presenting reference books that are not very well known, present full publication information.

```
Grimstead, David.  "Fuller, Margaret Sarah."  Encyclopedia of American
    Biography.  Ed. John A. Garraty.  New York: Harper, 1974.
```

A reprint of an older edition

When citing a reprint of an older edition—a paperback edition of a hardback book, for example—give the original publication date and then the date of the reprint.

Greenberg, Daniel S. <u>The Politics of Pure Science</u>. 1967. New York:
    NAL, 1971.

A pamphlet

<u>Existing Light Photography</u>. Rochester: Kodak, 1982.

A government publication

If no author is listed, treat the government agency as the author of the publication. Give the name of the government followed by the name of the agency. Underline the title, and include the publishing information that appears on the title page of the document.

United States. Dept. of State. <u>International Control of Atomic
    Energy: Growth of a Policy</u>. Washington: GPO, 1946.

A short story in an anthology

Faulkner, William. "A Rose for Emily." <u>To Read Literature</u>. Ed.
    Donald Hall. 2nd ed. New York: Holt, 1987. 4-10.

A short story in a collection

Stafford, Jean. "The Echo and the Nemesis." <u>The Collected Stories</u>.
    New York: Farrar, 1970. 35-53.

A short poem in a collection

Enclose the title of a short poem in quotation marks.

Pound, Ezra. "A Virginal." <u>Selected Poems of Ezra Pound</u>. New York:
    New Directions, 1957. 23.

A book-length poem

Underline the title of a book-length poem.

```
Eliot, T. S. The Waste Land. T. S. Eliot: Collected Poems 1909-1962.
     New York: Harcourt, 1963. 51-70.
```

A play in an anthology

```
Shakespeare, William. Othello, The Moor of Venice. Shakespeare: Six
     Plays and The Sonnets. Eds. Thomas Marc Parrott and Edward
     Hubler. New York: Scribner's, 1956.
```

Sample Citations—Articles

In general a citation for a periodical article contains the following information:

1. The author's name (last name first) followed by a period and two spaces
2. The title of the article, enclosed within quotation marks followed by a period and two spaces
3. The underlined title of the magazine or journal
4. The volume number
5. The date of publication, enclosed within parentheses, followed by a colon
6. The inclusive pagination of the full article, followed by a period.

However, when an article does not appear on consecutive pages—that is, it begins on page 30, skips to page 32, and ends on page 45—include only the first page of the article followed by a plus sign (30 + in this case).

The following examples illustrate variations on this format.

An article in a scholarly journal with continuous pagination

A journal has continuous pagination if the pagination runs consecutively from one issue to the next throughout an annual volume (for example one issue ends on page 252 and the next begins on page 253). In this case, you include the volume number of the journal in your citation.

```
LeGuin, Ursula K. "American Science Fiction and the Other." Science
     Fiction Studies 2 (1975): 208-10.
```

An article in a scholarly journal that has separate pagination

A citation for an article in a journal that begins with page 1 in each issue should include the volume number, a period, and then the issue number.

> Farrell, Thomas J. "Developing Literate Writing." <u>Basic Writing</u> 2.1
> (1978): 30-51.

An article in a weekly or biweekly magazine

To locate an article in a magazine, a reader needs a day, month, and year of publication, not the volume and issue numbers. In your citation, abbreviate all months except for May, June, and July.

> Cuomo, Mario. "Family Style." <u>New York</u> 12 May 1986: 84.

An unsigned article in a weekly or biweekly magazine

> "Solzhenitsyn: An Artist Becomes an Exile." <u>Time</u> 25 Feb. 1974: 34+.

An article in a monthly or bimonthly magazine

In a citation for a magazine published monthly or bimonthly, give the month and year, not the volume and issue numbers.

> Williamson, Ray. "Native Americans Were the First Astronomers."
> <u>Smithsonian</u> Oct. 1978: 78-85.
> Gaspen, Phyllis. "Indisposed to Medicine: The Women's Self-Help
> Movement." <u>The New Physicians</u> May-June 1980: 20-24.

An article in a daily newspaper

Give the name of the newspaper as it appears on the first page of the paper, but omit the article (<u>Washington Post</u>, not <u>The Washington Post</u>). Give the date the article appeared, the edition, and the section if each section is numbered separately, and the page or pages on which the article appears.

```
Boffey, Phillip M.  "Security and Science Collide on Data Flow."  Wall
    Street Journal 24 Jan. 1982, eastern ed.: 20.
"Madman Attacks Alligator."  Smithville Observer 14 August 1981, late
    ed., sec. 4: 5+.
```

An editorial

```
Rips, Michael D.  "Let's Junk the National Anthem."  Editorial.  New
    York Times 5 July 1986, natl. ed.: 23.
```

A review

After a reviewer's name and the title of the review (if it has one), write *Rev. of* followed by the work that is reviewed, a comma, the word *by*, and the author. If the review has no listed author, begin with the title of the review. If the review has neither an author nor a title, begin with *Rev. of* and use the title of the work that is reviewed as a guide when you alphabetize the entry.

```
Nilsen, Don L. F.  Rev. of American Tongue and Cheek: A Populist Guide
    to Our Language, by Jim Quinn.  College Composition and
    Communication 37 (1986): 107-108.
```

A letter to the editor

```
Bishop, Jennifer.  Letter.  Philadelphia Inquirer.  10 Dec. 1987: A26.
```

Sample Citations—Nonprint Sources

Computer software

Include the writer of the software, the title of the program followed by the label *Computer software*, the company, and the year of publication. In addition, include the computer for which the software was designed (IBM, Apple, etc.). If you do not know the writer, begin the citation with the name of the program.

```
Multiplan.  Computer software.  Microsoft, 1984.  Apple Macintosh.
```

Material from a computer service

Cite this material the way that you would any other article, but in addition, include the filing information provided by the computer service.

```
Williams, Jack. "A Revolution in Government Procurement." Harvard
     Business Review May-June 1985: 137+. DIALOG file 143, item
     128761 976230.
```

A lecture

Give the name of the lecturer, the title, the location, and the date on which the lecture took place. Include the sponsoring organization if there is one, and supply a descriptive label if the lecture has no title.

```
Abel, Robert. "Communication Theory and Film." Communications
     Colloquium, Dept. of Humanities and Communications, Drexel U,
     20 Oct. 1986.
```

A personal interview

```
Fuller, Buckminster. Personal interview. 17 Dec. 1980.
Davidowicz, Lucy. Telephone interview. 7 May 1985.
```

A personal letter

```
Walker, Alice. Letter to the author. 8 June 1986.
```

A film

Include the name of the film, the director, the distributor, the year, and any other information that you think is important. If you are emphasizing the contribution of any one person—the director, for example—begin with that person's name.

```
Lucas, George, dir. Return of the Jedi. With Mark Hamill, Harrison
     Ford, Carrie Fisher, and Billy Dee Williams. Twentieth Century
     Fox, 1983.
```

A videocassette

> <u>Arthur Miller</u>: The Crucible. Videocassette. Dir. William Schiff.
>   The Mosaic Group, 1987. 20 min.

A television or radio program

Include the name of the program (underlined), the network, the local station, the city, and the date of the program. You may also include other information that you think is important (the writers, for example). If an individual program in a series has a title, include it and put it in quotation marks.

> <u>Nothing to Fear: The Legacy of F.D.R.</u> Narr. John Hart. NBC. KNBC,
>   Los Angeles. 24 Jan. 1982.
> "The Greening of the Forests." <u>Life on Earth</u>. Narr. David
>   Attenborough. PBS. WHYY, Philadelphia. 26 Jan. 1982.

Explanatory Notes

Explanatory notes—commentary on sources or additional information on content that does not fit smoothly into the text—may be used along with parenthetical documentation and are indicated by a raised number in the text. The full text of these notes appears on the first full numbered page, entitled *Notes*, following the last page of the paper and before the list of works cited.

For more than one source

Use explanatory notes for references to numerous citations in a single reference. These references would be listed in the works cited section.

- **In the paper**

> Just as the German and Russian Jews had different religious practices,
> they also had different experiences becoming Americanized. [1]

- **In the note**

> [1] Glanz 37-38; Howe 72-77; Manners 50-52; and Glazer and Moynihan
> 89-93.

For explanations

Use notes to provide comments or explanations that are needed to clarify a point in the text.

- **In the paper**

  According to Robert Kimbrough, from the moment it was published, reviewers saw The Turn of the Screw as one of Henry James's most telling creations (169).[2]

- **In the note**

  [2] For typical early reactions to The Turn of the Screw see Phelps 17; Woolf 65-67; and Pattee 206-207.

- **In the paper**

  In recent years, Gothic novels have achieved great popularity.[3]

- **In the note**

  [3] Originally Gothic novels were works written in imitation of medieval romances and relied on ghosts, supernatural occurrences, and terror. They flourished in the late eighteenth and early nineteenth centuries.

THE CHICAGO FORMAT

The Chicago Manual of Style* uses notes that appear at the bottom of the page (footnotes) or at the end of the paper (endnotes) and bibliographic citations at the end of the paper. A bibliography at the end of a history paper is often annotated—that is, it contains a short summary for each work. The notes format uses a raised numeral at the end of the sentence in which you have either quoted or made reference to an idea or a piece of information from a source. This same number should appear at the beginning of the note. The first time you make reference to a work you use the full citation; *subsequent references* to the same work should list the author's last name, followed by a comma, a shortened version of the title, and a page number.

*The Chicago format follows the guidelines set in the *The Chicago Manual of Style*. 13th ed. Chicago: University of Chicago Press, 1982.

- First note on Espinoza

    1. J. M. Espinoza, First Expedition of Vargas in New Mexico, 1692
    (Albuquerque: University of New Mexico Press, 1940), 10-15.

- Bibliographic Form

    Espinoza, J. M. First Expedition of Vargas in New Mexico, 1692.
        Albuquerque: University of New Mexico Press, 1940.

- Subsequent Notes on Espinoza

    2. Espinoza, First Expedition of Vargas, 69.
    3. Espinoza, First Expedition, 70.

If you are required to use *footnotes,* be sure that the note numbers on a particular page of your paper correspond to the footnotes at the bottom of the page. *Endnotes* are all of your notes on a separate sheet at the end of the paper under the title *Notes.*

Sample Citations for Notes—Books

A book by one author

1. Herbert J. Gans, The Urban Villagers, 2nd ed. (New York: Free
Press, 1982), 100.

A book by two or three authors

2. James West Davidson and Mark Hamilton Lytle, After the
Fact: The Art of Historical Detection (New York: Alfred Knopf,
1982), 54.

A multivolume work

3. Kathleen Raine, Blake and Tradition (Princeton: Princeton
University Press, 1968), 1:100.

4. Will Durant and Ariel Durant, The Age of Napoleon: A History of
European Civilization from 1789 to 1815, vol. II of The Story of
Civilization (New York: Simon and Schuster, 1975), 90.

An edited book

> 5. William Bartram, The Travels of William Bartram, ed. Mark Van
> Doren (New York: Dover Press, 1955), 85.

An essay in an anthology

> 6. G. E. R. Lloyd, "Science and Mathematics," in The Legacy of
> Greece, ed. M. I. Finley (New York: Oxford University Press, 1981),
> 256-300.

An article in an encyclopedia

> 7. The Focal Encyclopedia of Photography, rev. ed. (1965), s.v.
> "Daguerreotype."
>
> 8. The Encyclopedia of Philosophy, 1967 ed., s.v. "Hobbes, Thomas"
> by R. S. Peters.

S.V. stands for *sub verbo*—under the word.

Sample Citations for Notes—Articles

An article in a scholarly journal with continuous pagination

> 1. John Huntington, "Science Fiction and the Future," College
> English 37 (Fall 1975): 340-58.

An article in a scholarly journal with separate pagination in each issue

> 2. R. G. Sipes, "War, Sports, and Aggression: An Empirical Test of
> Two Rival Theories," American Anthropologist 4, no. 2 (Spring
> 1973): 84.

An article in a weekly magazine

> 3. Sharon Bergley, "Redefining Intelligence," Newsweek, 14
> November 1983, 123.
>
> 4. "Solzhenitsyn: A Candle in the Wind," Time, 23 March 1970, 70.

An article in a monthly magazine

5. Lori Roll, "Careers in Engineering," Working Woman, November
1982, 62.

An article in a newspaper

6. Raymond Bonner, "A Guatemalan General's Rise to Power," New
York Times, 21 July 1982, A3.

Sample Citations for Bibliographies—Books

A book by one author

Gans, Herbert J. The Urban Villagers, 2nd ed. New York: Free Press,
1982.

A book by two or more authors

Davidson, James West and Mark Hamilton Lytle. After the Fact: The
Art of Historical Detection. New York: Alfred Knopf, 1982.

A multivolume work

Raine, Kathleen. Vol. 1 of Blake and Tradition. Princeton:
Princeton University Press, 1968.

Durant, Will and Ariel Durant. The Age of Napoleon: A History of
European Civilization from 1789 to 1815. Vol. II of The Story
of Civilization. New York: Simon and Schuster, 1975.

An edited book

Bartram, William. The Travels of William Bartram. Edited by Mark
Van Doren. New York: Dover Press, 1955.

An essay in an anthology

Lloyd, G. E. R. "Science and Mathematics." In The Legacy of
Greece, edited by M. I. Finley, 256-300. New York: Oxford
University Press, 1981.

An article in an encyclopedia (unsigned/signed)

> The Focal Encyclopedia of Photography, Rev. ed. (1965), s.v.
>
>   "Daguerreotype."
>
> The Encyclopedia of Philosophy. 1967 ed. s.v. "Hobbes, Thomas." by
>
>   R. S. Peters.

In a bibliography, these works are listed according to the name of the encyclopedia. The abbreviation s.v. stands for *sub verbo* (under the word). Most encyclopedias are arranged alphabetically according to key terms. Providing the key word allows your reader to find the appropriate entry.

Sample Citations for Bibliographies—Articles

An article in a scholarly journal with continuous pagination

> Huntington, John. "Science Fiction and the Future." College
>
>   English 37 (Fall 1975): 340-58.

An article in a scholarly journal with separate pagination in each issue

> Sipes, R. G. "War, Sports, and Aggression: An Empirical Test of Two
>
>   Rival Theories." American Anthropologist 4, no. 2 (Spring
>
>   1973): 65-84.

An article in a weekly magazine

> Bergley, Sharon. "Redefining Intelligence." Newsweek, 14 November
>
>   1983, 123.
>
> "Solzhenitsyn: A Candle in the Wind." Time, 23 March 1970, 70.

An article in a monthly magazine

> Roll, Lori. "Careers in Engineering." Working Woman, November
>
>   1982, 62.

An article in a newspaper

> Bonner, Raymond. "A Guatemalan General's Rise to Power." New York
>
>   Times, 21 July 1982, A3.

Other Humanities Formats

Your instructor may require a format other than MLA or Chicago style. Most style manuals are readily available in the reference sections of libraries. *A Manual for Writers of Term Papers, Theses, and Dissertations* by Kate L. Turabian (The University of Chicago Press 1973) and *Writing About Music: A Style Book for Reports and Theses* by Demar B. Irvine (The University of Washington Press, 1968) are two style manuals that use formats based on the Chicago style.

Sample Humanities Papers

The following papers illustrate the MLA and Chicago styles of documentation. The first two papers—"Mark Twain: Civil War Deserter?" and "Rudolfo Anaya's *Bless Me, Ultima*: A Microcosmic Representation of Chicano Literature"—use the MLA format. The third paper "Anglo-American Policy in the Caribbean," follows the Chicago format.

SAMPLE HUMANITIES PAPER: MLA FORMAT
[No title page; with outline]

Olivia Guest

Professor Dugan

English 102

April 30, 1987

1″ *from top*
of page

Mark Twain: Civil War Deserter?

Topic outline
of student's
paper

I. Introduction--Shannon's accusations about Twain's
    cowardice during the Civil War

II. Explanation in the autobiography

III. Descriptions in "History"

    A. Humorous description

    B. Indictment of war

IV. Accusation of childishness

    A. Van Wyck Brooks

    B. New York Times

    C. Support from "History"

V. Antiwar explanation

    A. Support of explanation

        1. Justin Kaplan

        2. J. Stanley Mattson

    B. Refutation of explanation--Maxwell Geismar

VI. Divided sympathies

    A. Twain's divided sympathy

        1. Connection to the South

        2. Connection to the North

Guest ii

      B. Missouri's divided sympathy

          1. Minimal interest in the war

          2. Opposition to secession

          3. Confusion illustrated in "History"

VII.   Other influences

      A. Interest in the continent

      B. Orion's influence

VIII. Desertion as a common occurrence

      A. Bell Wiley's statistics

      B. Twain's description of camp life

Guest 1   *½" from top
                                                                of page*

Mark Twain: Civil War Deserter?   *centered title*

  On January 25, 1940, Representative Shannon of

Missouri insisted that his state did not want any of the

recently issued stamps commemorating Mark Twain. According   *background
                                                                     established*
to Shannon, Twain had disgraced Missouri during the Civil

War. Soon after Twain had joined the Confederate forces

under a Colonel Jack Burbridge and had been made a

lieutenant, Twain deserted. In Shannon's version of what

had happened, "A Minie ball came whizzing past his ears, and   *brackets to
                                                                       indicate
[Twain] started running. He ran; and, oh, how fast he did   insertion*

run. He never stopped until he got to Keokuk, Iowa. Colonel

Burbridge fought 4 years in the Southern Army; Mark Twain

about 4 minutes." Shannon concluded his criticism by

quoting Captain Billy Ely, who had been company commander of

the Burbridge Brigade, "I can say to my fellow Missourians

that we had but one coward in our whole group, and his name

was Samuel L. Clemens" (Cong. Rec. 698-99).

  Shannon's version of Mark Twain's military career is

not completely accurate, but it does bring up some

interesting questions. What was Twain's position during   *purpose: to
                                                                       find out why
the Civil War? Why did he desert? When we look to Twain   Twain
                                                                       deserted*
himself, we get very little reliable information. In his

autobiography we learn that the war interrupted his career

*name and
page number
on every page*

as a river pilot. Then he devotes only two sentences to the
whole war episode:

> In June I joined the Confederates in Ralls
> County, Missouri, as a second Lieutenant under
> General Tom Harris and came near having the
> distinction of being captured by Colonel
> Ulysses S. Grant. I resigned after two weeks'
> service in the field, explaining that I was
> "incapacitated by fatigue" through persistent
> retreating. (102)

*quotation of
more than 4
lines indented
10 spaces from
left margin*

*page number
after period
and 2 spaces*

Another version of his career as a soldier appeared
first in 1884 in Century Magazine as "The Private History of
a Campaign That Failed." However colorful and interesting
this account, it is probably more fictional than factual.
According to William J. Kimball, "Exactly what happened in
the summer of 1861 is probably beyond recovery, but the
'History' is obviously not an accurate account" (382). In
the tale Twain tells of kids who join together to play
soldier in a real war. They spend their time for the most
part avoiding the Union forces they are supposed to be
locating. The story contains several very humorous
descriptions: the pretentious Dunlap, who changed his name
to d'Un Lap; the uncooperative mules and horses, which
constantly threw and bit their riders; the men, who rolled
down hills in mud, slept in a corn crib, and were captured

*quotation
marks around
a short
quotation*

Guest 3

by dogs ("the most mortifying spectacle of the Civil War").
No one would cook, and no one would take orders.

In addition to the humor, the story also contains a
very moving and dark episode in which Sam Clemens thinks
that he has shot an innocent stranger:

> And it seemed an epitome of war; that all war
> must be just that--the killing of strangers
> against whom you feel no personal animosity;
> strangers whom, in other circumstances, you
> would help if you found them in trouble, and who
> would help you if you needed it. (263)

Several people have tried to explain Mark Twain's war
experiences with less prejudice than Representative
Shannon. In fact, together they help to sort out the
confusion we feel about Twain's actions.

*transitional
paragraph*

Van Wyck Brooks in The Ordeal of Mark Twain blames
Twain's desertion on an "infantile frame of mind." Brooks
maintains that Twain's independence from his mother's
"leading strings" was so ill developed that he "slipped back
into the boy he had been before." Brooks writes that we can
see this trait in the "History":

*combination
of three
sources by
paraphrasing
and quoting*

> . . . a singular childishness, a sort of
> infantility, in fact that is very hard to
> reconcile with the character of any man of
> twenty-six and especially one who, a few weeks

Guest 4

before, had been a river "sovereign," the
steamboat, a worshipper of energy and
purpose. (74-75)

In the New York Times a response to Representative Shannon's
attack also points out that although at the time of his
desertion Twain was 26, "mentally he was not yet 21" ("Ranger
of Hannibal"). In "History," one of Twain's remarks supports
this view. After he has become disillusioned with war, Twain
comments, "It seemed to me that I was not rightly equipped
for this awful business; that war was intended for men, and I
for a child's nurse" (263). He also writes that the war had
not yet turned the "green recruits" from "rabbits into
soldiers" (265).

Justin Kaplan in his biography Mr. Clemens and Mark
Twain writes that the episode of the killing of the stranger
in "History" gave Twain a justification to desert. Now
because of the nightmarish killing, even though fictional,
Twain was able to condemn war as dreadful. Thus, to Kaplan
the story is intended to help remove the burden of guilt
(322-25). J. Stanley Mattson also supports the view that
the story is antiwar and that Twain is a pacifist. He
writes, "It directs an arsenal of grape-shot at the entire
concept of the glory of war" (794). Maxwell Geismar in Mark
Twain: An American Prophet argues that although the story
brings out the horror of war, its overall intention is to be

*title used
when author
unknown*

*two
conflicting
sources*

Guest 5

humorous--"humor, yes. Guilt, no!" And Mark Twain left
service with about half of the company simply because the
"war was a disappointment" (129-30).

parentheses inside the period

Perhaps more plausible than desertion because of
exhaustion, childishness, or the inhumanity of war are
explanations based on considerations of family, friends, and
locality. Twain's sympathies leaned toward the South; he
had recently spent time in Louisiana. When he returned to
Missouri, he hid out for a while fearing he would be forced
to pilot a Union gunboat. Twain's aunt wrote that when a
friend suggested a Confederate company, Twain "accepted at
once" (Webster 60). However, his brother Orion, to whom
Twain was very close, favored the Union side. Showing how
divided Mark Twain was, his aunt wrote the following:

transitional sentence

author's name in parentheses when not in text

> He loved his country's flag and all that it
> symbolized. . . . I know he would gladly have
> given his life for his country, but he was a
> Southerner, his friends were all Southern, his
> sympathies were with the South. It was the same
> problem that Robert E. Lee and thousands
> faced. (Webster 62)

The divided sympathies and possible indifference of
Twain were typical of the feeling in Missouri as a whole.
The interest in the war was minimal; "most Missourians
probably would gladly have watched the war from the

sidelines, waiting to study the meaning of its outcome"
(Nagel 128). Voters (70 percent) favored compromise.
Lincoln received only 10 percent of the votes. In a special
1861 convention, only 30,000 votes out of 140,000 cast
favored secession. Despite the opposition, Missouri
entered the war favoring the Union; three-fourths of the
soldiers fought for the Union (Nagel 128-29). At the
beginning of the "History" Twain writes of "a good deal of
confusion in men's minds" and "a good deal of unsettledness,
of leading first this way, then that, then the other way"
(243). He tells that his pilot-mate and he were "strong for
the Union." Then they both became rebels. Later the friend
switched again and was piloting a federal gunboat (244).

Henry Seidel Canby expresses Twain's dilemma this
way: Twain was "Southern in manners and Northern in mind."
But Canby offers another dimension to the problem. Twain
was really not interested in North or South, but it was "the
continent that excited and persuaded him" (26). About this
same time, Twain's brother Orion, a lawyer who had
campaigned to get Lincoln elected President, got appointed
Secretary of the Nevada Territory. When Orion left for
Nevada, Twain went with him (Mack 47-49). Delancey Ferguson
reports that "Orion wanted to stop his brother's dallying
with the Southern cause" (65).

To people today, desertion seems a terrible crime and

Guest 7

cowardly act. But during the Civil War, it was very common.
Bell Wiley in The Common Soldier of the Civil War points out
that many soldiers unlawfully left camp. He estimates
deserters at 100,000 for the Confederate forces and 200,000
for the Federals. Wiley attributes the large numbers of
desertions to the monotony of camp life (63). Twain
supports this point in "History":

> We stayed several days at Mason's; and after all
> these years the memory of the dulness [sic], the
> stillness, and lifelessness of that slumberous
> farm-house still oppresses my spirit as with a
> sense of the presence of death and mourning.
> There was nothing to do, nothing to think about;
> there was no interest in life. (257)

sic in brackets to indicate spelling error in the original

From a historical perspective, Twain's desertion was
not unusual. Because of Twain's closeness to Orion, the
decision to leave for Nevada was not surprising. No one
should hastily condemn Twain without considering the
complexity of the desertion.

conclusion — reasons for Twain's desertion were complex

Guest 8

Works Cited

Brooks, Van Wyck. The Ordeal of Mark Twain. New York:

Dutton, 1933.

Canby, Henry Seidel. Turn West, Turn East: Mark Twain and

Henry James. Boston: Houghton, 1951.

Clemens, Samuel L. The Autobiography of Mark Twain. Ed.

Charles Neider. New York: Harper, 1959.

---. "The Private History of a Campaign That Failed." The

American Claimant and Other Stories and Sketches.

New York: Harper, 1897.

Cong. Rec. 25 Jan. 1940: 698-99.

Ferguson, Delancey. Mark Twain: Man and Legend.

Indianapolis: Bobbs, 1943.

Geismar, Maxwell. Mark Twain: An American Prophet. Boston:

Houghton, 1970.

Kaplan, Justin. Mr. Clemens and Mark Twain. 1966. New

York: Pocket, 1968.

Kimball, William J. "Samuel Clemens as a Confederate

Soldier: Some Observations about 'The Private History

of a Campaign That Failed.'" Studies in Short Fiction

5 (1968): 382-84.

Mack, Effie Mona. Mark Twain in Nevada. New York:

Scribner's, 1947.

all material double-spaced

hyphens to indicate same author as above

volume, year, pages

Guest 9

Mattson, J. Stanley. "Mark Twain on War and Peace: The

    Missouri Rebel and 'The Campaign That Failed.'"

    American Quarterly 20 (1968): 785-94.

Nagel, Paul C. Missouri: A Bicentennial History. New York:

    Norton, 1977.

"Ranger of Hannibal." New York Times 7 Feb. 1940: 20.   *author
                                                                  unknown;
Webster, Samuel Charles, ed. Mark Twain, Business Man.   work
                                                                  alphabetized
    Boston: Little, 1946.   by title*

Wiley, Bell. The Common Soldier of the Civil War. New

    York: Scribner's, 1975.

SAMPLE HUMANITIES PAPER: MLA FORMAT
[With title page, no outline]

Rudolfo Anaya's Bless Me, Ultima:

A Microcosmic Representation of Chicano Literature

by

Jennifer Flemming

English 3112

Dr. Jussawalla

May 12, 1986

Rudolfo Anaya's Bless Me, Ultima:

A Microcosmic Representation of Chicano Literature

      Chicano authors have sometimes been called "noble
savages" and they have been denied credit and recognition in
the field of literature and culture. Some scholars and
teachers consider Chicano literature as "newly emerged"
from recent political developments and therefore lacking in
maturity and universal appeal, although others have traced
its growth and development in the Southwest since the 16th
century. The fact that most Chicano literature is based on
social protest and is associated with political events also
elicits less than positive responses from literary critics.
The political nature of the literature causes it to be
viewed as not quite legitimate. However, Chicano literature
is neither "newly emerged" and thus lacking in maturity, nor
merely reflective of recent socio-political movements. On
the contrary, Chicano literature--writing done by American
Hispanics--not only records the Mexican-American experience
in the American Southwest but also demonstrates the
universality of that experience. Rudolfo Anaya's Bless Me,
Ultima, which records the Mexican-American experience while
describing the emotions universal to most 10-year-old boys,
exemplifies the dual role of the best Chicano literature.

Flemming 2

Paredes and Paredes's definition of Chicano
literature ties it to the Chicano's key role in the cultural
development of the American Southwest:

> People like to record their experiences;
> Mexican-Americans have been no exception. They
> have had much to write about. Their lives have
> sometimes been stormy and often tragic, but
> always vital and intriguing. It is hardly
> surprising that Mexican-Americans have literary
> talents, for they are heirs to the European
> civilization of Spain and the Indian
> civilizations of Mexico both of which produced
> great poets and storytellers. Furthermore,
> they have also been in contact with the history
> and literature of the United States. . . . (1)

This connection of the development of the literature
with the locale is made by Luis Leal in his article,
"Mexican American Literature: A Historical Perspective,"
when he notes that Chicano literature had its origin when
the Southwest was settled by the inhabitants of Mexico
during colonial times (22). He emphasizes that the
literature originated both from the contact of the colonial
Mexicans with the Native Americans and from the contact with
the Anglo culture that was moving westward. In fact, many
of the themes of Chicano literature emphasize the coming in

Flemming 3

contact of two vastly different cultures. This is
particularly true of Anaya's Bless Me, Ultima, which also
reflects the universal emotions and feelings generated as a
result of the clash of cultures.

A recording of the experience of the Southwest is
found in Anaya's Bless Me, Ultima, which ultimately
universal themes of initiation and maturation (Novoa,
"Themes"). In his novel about the rites of passage of a
young boy (Antonio) from innocent adolescence to the
ambiguous and morally corrupt adult world, the author
expresses his culture's indigenous beliefs, myths, and
legends.

Antonio's father tells him of the coming of the
Spanish colonizers to the Valley, their contact with the
American Indian culture which Ultima--an older grandmother
figure--exemplifies, and the changes brought about in the
village and the town by the coming of the Tejanos. Yet the
theme is universal, transcending the boundaries of his
village. The events that result from the clash between the
old and the new could take place anywhere in the world
because they deal with religious hatred and with the
conflicts between different ways of life.

The novel relates the story of a young boy and his
friendship with a curandera (charlatan) named Ultima who
comes to live with Antonio and his family. The arrival

of Ultima has an enormous impact on him because he feels a
kinship with her. For instance, through Ultima, Antonio--
now nicknamed Tony--comes in contact with the local Indian
religions. Ultima teaches him about herbs and their potency
in creating conditions often associated with magic. She
also introduces Antonio to Narcisso, the Indian who teaches
him the myth of the Golden Carp: "The people who killed the
carp of the river . . . were punished by being turned into
fish themselves. After that happened many years later, a
new people came to live in this valley" (Anaya 110). This
myth encapsulates the history of the Indian people, the
Hispanic colonizers, and the Anglo settlers of New Mexico.
Tony sees the reflection of the myth in his day-to-day life.
The Indians and the Hispanics of the valley are gradually
replaced by the "new people," the Anglos. This stirs in him
deep love for his land, his people, and his lifestyle.

But at school he is teased for believing in these
myths. His classmates, who have already laughed at his lunch
of tortillas and his inability to speak English, taunt him
about Ultima. Calling her a <u>bruja</u> (witch) they say, "Hey,
Tony, can you make the ball disappear?" "Hey, Tony, do some
magic" (Anaya 102). Tony suffers the angst of a ten-year-old
taunted by these voices. He begins to suffer doubts about
his identity and the rightness of his beliefs.

At the end of the book, when Ultima is killed by the

townspeople for being a witch, Antonio falls to his knees to
pray for her and in facing her death reaches his maturation.
He knows what is right for him: "I praised the beauty of the
Golden Carp" (Anaya 244).

Anaya has said, "When people ask me where my roots
are, I look down at my feet. . . . They are here, in New
Mexico, in the Southwest" (Novoa, Chicano Authors 185). The
author's message is clear and undeniable: one must go back
to one's roots, despite the conflicting pull of
Americanization. It is the same message of faith and hope,
which Ultima, on her deathbed, gives to Antonio: learn to
accept life's experiences and feel the strength of who you
are. In the character of Ultima, however, Anaya has created
a symbol of beauty, harmony, understanding, and the power of
goodness that transcends the limits of time and space and
religious beliefs.

From the above examples it can be seen that Anaya is
capable of producing Chicano literature that has universal
appeal and themes. Anaya's novel records the Mexican-
American experience of the Southwest while creating
characters and portraying emotions of universal appeal.
The social protest against Americanization is secondary to
the treatment of myth and emotions.

Chicano literature cannot be considered just a
by-product of the recent struggle for civil rights. This is

Flemming 6

not to minimize or deny the effects of the Chicano political
movement and the new sense of awareness and direction that
it has sparked (which includes the proliferation of Chicano
literary texts). Although Chicano literature may appear to
emphasize social protest and criticism of the dominant
Anglo culture, or seem to be introspectively searching for
self-definition, it will not be found lacking in universal
appeal (Leal 42).

Flemming 7

Works Cited

Anaya, Rudolfo. Bless Me, Ultima. Berkeley: Tonatiuh, 1972.

Jimenez, Francisco. The Identification and Analysis of
    Chicano Literature. New York: Bilingual, 1979.

Leal, Luis, et al. A Decade of Chicano Literature. Santa
    Barbara: La Causa, 1982.

---. "Mexican American Literature: A Historical
    Perspective." Modern Chicano Writers. Eds. Joseph
    Sommers and Tomas Ybarra-Fausto. Englewood Cliffs:
    Prentice, 1979. 18-40.

Martinez, Julio A. and Francisco A. Lomeli. Chicano
    Literature: A Reference Guide. Westport: Greenwood,
    1985.

Novoa, Juan-Bruce. "Themes in Rudolfo Anaya's Work." Talk
    given at New Mexico State University. Las Cruces,
    11 Apr. 1987.

---. Chicano Authors: Inquiry by Interview. Austin: U of
    Texas P, 1980.

Paredes, Americo and Raymond Paredes. Mexican-American
    Authors. Boston: Houghton, 1973.

SAMPLE HUMANITIES PAPER: CHICAGO FORMAT

Anglo-American Policy in the Caribbean

Thomas C. Howard

History Department

February, 1989

Anglo-American Policy in the Caribbean

The formal colonial empire of Britain in the
Caribbean long rested near the informal American imperial
presence. Eventually the British flag was lowered here as
well, succumbing to nationalistic demands, metropolitan
weariness, and, as emphasized here, international realities.
Britain's role in the region diminished. In relinquishing
control, Britain became here, as elsewhere in the world, the
frequently ambivalent junior partner in what seemed to be
the emerging American world system. Here, however, she
could at least cushion the trauma of decline with illusions
about the strength and durability of her "special
relationship" with her former colonies. Even so, American
anti-colonialism can be seen as a force in the break up of
the British West Indian Empire after 1945.

Historically the British West Indian colonies
represented remnants of the Old Empire. In the mercantilist
system of the 17th and 18th centuries, they had indeed been
most valuable. The economics of sugar and abolitionism and
the needs of the Victorian free trade empire all left the
British West Indies in a state of neglect for many years and
held back political development. Neglect in the West Indies,
however, was widespread. Despite various calls for

corrective action, little was done until the 1930s and then
only in reaction to a number of serious civil disturbances
and strikes stemming from the economic dislocations of the
depression. Britain was able to carry on this policy of
benign neglect for so long largely because of the
hemispheric dominance of the United States, a reality
formally acknowledged in 1902 with the Hay-Pauncefote
Treaties,[1] which solidified regional understanding with
the United States.

In the years after the first World War, policymakers
suspected more and more that the empire might be "made of
porcelain."[2] Cracks did begin to appear despite efforts to
use diplomacy, influence, and economics to maintain the
status quo. In 1941 these neglected islands served as bases
for the United States and thus started the war-time
partnership which temporarily revived the entire empire.

It was a unique situation. Here suddenly were
colonies within colonies--American bases, air strips, and
service facilities being constructed on British colonial
soil, all with vast potential for friction and the spread of
American influence. What better place to find examples of
colonial repression to feed the flames of renewed American
anti-imperialism than right here in the United States's
"own backyard"? What better place for Britain to attempt to
brush up its colonial image than through development

schemes for the empire? What better place for emerging
nationalist movements to take advantage of the resurgence of
American anti-colonial sentiments as articulated through the
Atlantic Charter and subsequent wartime statements of
principle? In short, the factor of American anti-imperialism,
which was later to influence events in India, the Middle
East, and Africa, was first tested in the Caribbean.

So serious, in fact, were anxieties in some quarters in
Britain about American encroachments in the region by January
1942, that Churchill sent a personal appeal to Roosevelt
reminding him of his promise to make some statement
confirming "that there would be no question of transfer to
the United States of the British West Indian colonies, either
under the bases agreement or otherwise."[3] Although Roosevelt
agreed to such an assurance, Anglo-American tensions over the
future of the region did not disappear. Largely because of
these tensions, in fact, the Anglo-Caribbean Commission was
created in 1942. Enthusiastically promoted by the
Americans and consented to reluctantly on the British side,
this commission acquired unexpected importance, not only as
a functioning regional commission, but as a significant
factor in wider Anglo-American colonial discussion both
during and after the war. Certainly it provided a ready
forum for American criticism. This criticism was in part
responsible for a new Colonial Office resolve for genuine

colonial reform and development, including political
reforms which would lead eventually to self-government.
The needs of the region had been abundantly revealed by the
work of a royal commission in 1938-1939. The full text of
these recommendations, the Moyne Report, was not revealed
until 1945, but its stark portrayal of West Indian problems
served as the principal wartime moral incentive leading to
the Colonial Development and Welfare acts of the 1940s and
1950s. [4] The West Indies, therefore, served as a microcosm
of developments which later touched the empire as a whole.

In the immediate post-war period, many of the British
suspicions behind Churchill's 1942 message seemed well on
the way to fulfillment. In the Caribbean, although the
United States had kept its pledge not to annex Britain's
colonies, the American influence was more evident than
ever. Here, in fact, could be found quite early almost all
of the ingredients that were to form the global themes of
the second half of the century, not the least of which was
American imperialism as anti-communism.

Notes

1.　David Weigall, Britain and the World, 1815-1986 (New York: Oxford University Press, 1987), 107.

2.　John Gallagher, "The Decline, Revival, and Fall of the British Empire," in The Decline, Revival, and Fall of the British Empire, ed. Anil Seal (Cambridge: Cambridge University Press, 1982), 84.

3.　Warren F. Kimball, ed., Churchill and Roosevelt: Their Complete Correspondence (Princeton: Princeton University Press, 1984), 1:232.

4.　Lord Moyne (Chairman), West India: Royal Commission Report (London: HMSO, 1945).

Bibliography

Gallagher, John. "The Decline, Revival, and Fall of the
    British Empire." In The Decline, Revival, and Fall of
    the British Empire, edited by Anil Seal, 60-95.
    Cambridge: Cambridge University Press, 1982.

Kimball, Warren F., ed. Churchill and Roosevelt: Their
    Complete Correspondence. Princeton: Princeton
    University Press, 1984.

Moyne, Lord (Chairman). West India: Royal Commission
    Report. London: HMSO, 1945.

Weigall, David. Britain and the World, 1815-1986. New
    York: Oxford University Press, 1987.

WRITING IN THE SOCIAL SCIENCES

The social sciences include the following subject areas: anthropology, business, economics, education, political science, psychology, social work, and sociology. Writing in the social sciences differs from writing in the humanities in that it often casts information into particular formats, such as the case study. The case study is the dominant form for the presentation of information in psychology, sociology, anthropology, and political science, where it can examine an individual patient's case, the dynamics of a group, or the functioning of a political organization.

RESEARCH SOURCES

Although library research is an important component of research in the social sciences, the researcher is less bound to the library and can move out into field work with greater ease. Social scientists survey attitudes, record responses, and interview subjects. Because so much of their data is numerical, reported in tables and charts, it is essential for a social scientist to know how to read and interpret such figures. Much of your library research in social science disciplines will depend on abstracting information from such tables and charts. Therefore, general reference sources like yearbooks and almanacs may be particularly useful.

Specialized Library Sources

The following reference sources are useful in a variety of social science disciplines.

ASI Index (American Statistics Institute)
Encyclopedia of Black America
Handbook of North American Indians
Human Resources Abstracts
International Bibliography of the Social Sciences
International Encyclopedia of the Social Sciences
PAIS (Public Affairs Information Service)
Population Index
Social Sciences Citation Index

The following reference sources are most often used for research in specific disciplines.

Anthropology
Abstracts in Anthropology
Anthropological Index

Business and Economics
Business Periodicals Index

Criminal Justice
Abstracts on Criminology and Penology
Abstracts on Police Science
Criminal Justice Abstracts
Criminal Justice Periodicals Index

Education
Dictionary of Education
Education Index
Encyclopedia of Educational Research

Political Science
ABC Political Science
CIS Index (Congressional Information Service)
Combined Retrospective Index to Journals in Political Science
Encyclopedia of Modern World Politics
Encyclopedia of the Third World
Foreign Affairs Bibliography
Information Services on Latin America
International Political Science Abstracts
United States Political Science Documents
U.S. Serial Set Index

Psychology
Author Index to Psychological Index and Psychological Abstracts
Contemporary Psychology
Cumulative Subject Index to Psychological Abstracts
Encyclopedia of Psychology
Psychological Abstracts

Sociology
Poverty and Human Resources Abstracts
Rural Sociology Abstracts
Sage Family Studies Abstracts
Sociological Abstracts

Government Documents. Government documents are important resources for social scientists. They contain the most complete and up-to-date facts and figures necessary for any social analysis. Varied information—from technical, scientific, and medical information to everyday information on home safety for children—can be found in government documents.

Government documents can be searched through the *Monthly Catalog,* which contains the list of documents published that month together with a subject index. Other indexes include *The Congressional Information Service Index, The American Statistics Index,* and *The Index to U.S. Government Periodicals.*

Newspaper Articles. Newspaper articles are particularly useful sources for researching subjects in political science, history, economics, business, or social work. Students usually rely on the *New York Times,* which has indexes available both in print and on microfilm. However, for newspaper information from across the country, a handy and useful source is *Newsbank. Newsbank,* like the government's *Monthly Catalog,* provides subject headings under the appropriate government agencies. For instance, articles on child abuse are likely to be listed under Health and Human Services. Older articles will be listed in older *Newsbanks* under Health, Education, and Welfare. Once you find the subject area, *Newsbank* provides a microcard/microfiche number. On that microfiche you will find articles from around the country on your subject.

Specialized Databases for Computer Searches

Many of the print sources cited above have electronic counterparts. Some of the more widely used databases for social science disciplines include *Cendata, Business Periodicals Index, Social Sciences Index, PsycINFO, ERIC, Social Scisearch, Sociological Abstracts, Information Science Abstracts, PAIS International, Population Bibliography, Economic Literature Index, BI/INFORM, Legal Resources Index, Management Contents, Trade and Industry Index,* and *PTS F + S Indexes.*

Non-Library Sources

Interviews, questionnaires, surveys, and observation of the behavior of various groups and individuals are some of the important non-library sources in social science research. Assignments given by professors may ask you to use your classmates as subjects for questionnaires (see "Assignments in Academic Writing"). In political science your teacher may ask you to interview a sample of college students and classify them as conservative, liberal, or radical. You may be asked to poll each group to find out college students' attitudes on nuclear energy, chemical waste disposal, the question of the homeless, and other issues that affect them. If you were writing a paper on gifted programs in education, in addition to library research on the issue you might want to observe two classes—one of gifted students and one of students not participating in the gifted program. You might also want to interview students, teachers, or parents. In psychology and social work your research may rely on the observations of clients and patients and be written up as a case study (see page 72).

ASSIGNMENTS IN THE SOCIAL SCIENCES

Proposals

Proposals, often the first stage of any research project, help to clarify and focus a research project.

In a proposal you must argue for your subject. If a proposal is to be accepted by some funding agency from whom you expect some money, you have to sell them on your idea. This means that you have to learn to put the argument of your research project up front and defend it. In the process you must strictly adhere to any specifications outlined in the request for proposals issued by the grant-giving agency.

Many proposals contain a number of the following components.

• **Cover Sheet:** State your name, the title of your project, and to whom your proposal is submitted. Providing a short title will help you express your subject concisely. Thinking about whom your proposal is submitted to will help you focus on your audience. Usually another line is added on this sheet that states the reason for the submission of the proposal—for example, a request for funding or facilities.

```
                  Advantages of the Maquiladora Project
                             in El Paso


      Submitted to: The Committee on U.S.-Mexico Labor Relations
         For: Grant to Research the Benefits of Maquiladora
                        Employment to El Paso
                          by Laura Talamantes
```

• **Abstract:** Usually on a separate page, the abstract provides a short summary of your proposal. (See page 109 for information about writing abstracts.)
• **Statement of Purpose:** Essentially, this is your thesis statement. It states the purpose of your research project—for example, "The Maquiladora Project is an industrial development program which relies on international cooperation with Mexican industries to utilize Mexican labor while boosting the employment of U.S. white collar workers."

- **Background of the Problem:** This section should explain why your perspective on your topic is important. It is usually a paragraph that uses comparisons and contrasts with previous research, and indicates the need for your specific research.
- **Rationale:** This section, which justifies further the need for your research project, should be as persuasive as you can make it. Why is your research project justified? What causes it to be important at this time?
- **Statement of Qualification:** This section demonstrates why you are uniquely qualified to carry out the research and what special qualities you bring to your work.
- **Literature Survey:** This can be a brief survey of the information you have looked at that justifies the need for your project and shows the uniqueness of your point of view. In a real-world proposal, it needs to be fairly complete, as it helps to establish the writer's credibility as a researcher.
- **Research Methods:** This paragraph describes the exact methods you will use in carrying out your research and the materials you will need; in general, it demonstrates the soundness of your method.
- **Timetable:** States the time estimate for carrying out the project.
- **Budget:** Where applicable, estimates the costs for carrying out the research.
- **Conclusions/Applications:** Restates the importance of your project.

A proposal is usually sent with a cover letter, called a letter of transmittal, which follows business letter format. It is also accompanied by a brief résumé, one that lists only your qualifications for the project. This résumé summarizes your relevant work experience and accomplishments and reinforces your qualifications as presented in the statement of qualification.

Case Studies

Case studies are usually informative, describing the problem at hand and presenting solutions or treatments. They all essentially follow the same format: the statement of the problem, the background of the problem, the methods or processes of the solutions, the conclusions arrived at, and suggestions for improvement or future recommendations. Different disciplines make different uses of case studies. In political science, deliberations in policy-making and decision-making are subject to the case study methodology. Foreign policy negotiations, for instance, are described and written up as case studies. Issue analyses such as "Should government control the media?" can also be written as case studies.

In psychology, social work, and educational psychology or counseling the case study is an observation of an individual and his interaction with a certain agency. Such a case study usually involves describing the behavior of an individual or a group and outlining the steps to be taken in solving the problem that presents itself to the caseworker or researcher.

The case study that examines a problem in a group or in an environmental context follows the same format. Here is the introduction to a case study based on a social work student's assignment to observe one client.

> Mona Freeman, a 14-year-old girl, was brought to the Denver Children's Residential Treatment Center by her 70-year-old, devoutly religious adoptive mother. Both were personable, verbal, and neatly groomed. The presenting problem was seen differently by various members of the client system: Mrs. Freeman described Mona's "several years of behavioral problems," including "lying, stealing, and being boy crazy." Mona viewed herself as a "disappointment" and wanted "time to think." She had been expelled from the local Seventh Day Adventist School for being truant and defiant several months earlier and had been attending public school. The examining psychiatrist diagnosed a conduct disorder but saw no intellectual, physical, or emotional disabilities. He predicted that Mona probably would not be able to continue to live in "such an extreme disciplinary environment" as the home of Mrs. Freeman because she had lived for the years from seven until twelve with her natural father in Boston, Massachusetts—a fact which was described as a "kidnapping" by Mrs. Freeman. The psychiatrist mentioned some "depression" and attributed it to Mona's inability to fit in her current environment and the loss of life with her father in Boston.

CONVENTIONS OF STYLE AND FORMAT

Social science writing tends to use a technical vocabulary. For instance, in the social work case study, the student speaks of "the presenting problem," which is simply the reason the "subject," Mona, was brought to the Denver Children's Facility. Since you are speaking to specialists when you write papers in these disciplines, it is important to use the vocabulary of the field. Also, in describing charts and figures, it is important to use familiar statistical terms, such as means, percentages, chi squares, and other terms in the vocabulary of statistical analysis. But it is also important to explain in plain English what those percentages, means, and standard deviations mean in terms of your analysis.

The social science paper format typically uses internal headings (for example, Statement of Problem, Background of Problem, Description of Problem, Solutions, and Conclusion). Unlike the humanities paper, each section of a social science paper is written as a complete entity with a beginning and an end so that it can be read separately, out of context, and still make complete sense. The body of the paper may present charts or figures (graphs, maps, photographs, flow charts) as well as a discussion of those figures. Numerical data, such as statistics, are frequently presented in tabular form.

DOCUMENTATION FORMATS

Documentation format in the social sciences is more uniform than in the humanities or the sciences. The disciplines and journals in the social sciences almost uniformly use the documentation style of the American Psychological Association's *Publication Manual*.

THE APA FORMAT*

APA format, which is used extensively in the social sciences, relies on short references—consisting of the last name of the author and the year of publication—inserted within the text. These references are keyed to an alphabetical list of references that follows the paper.

Parenthetical References in the Text

One author

The APA format calls for a comma between the name and the date, whereas MLA format does not.

> One study of stress in the workplace (Weisberg, 1983) shows a
> correlation between . . .

As with MLA style, you do not include in the parenthetical reference information that appears in the text.

> In his study Weisberg (1983) shows a correlation . . . (author's
> name in text)

> In Weisberg's 1983 study of stress in the workplace . . . (author's
> name and date in text)

Two publications by same author(s), same year

If you cite two or more publications by the same author that appeared the same year, the first is designated *a*, the second *b* (e.g., Weisberg, 1983a and Weisberg, 1983b),

---

*APA documentation format follows the guidelines set in the *Publication Manual of the American Psychological Association*. 3rd ed. Washington, D.C.: APA, 1983.

and so on. These letter designations also appear in the reference list that follows the text of your paper.

He completed his next study of stress (Weisberg, 1983b) . . .

A publication by two or more authors

When a work has two authors, both names are cited.

There is a current and growing concern over the use of psychological testing in elementary schools (Albright & Glennon, 1982).

If a work has more than two authors but fewer than six authors, mention all names in the first reference, and in subsequent references cite the first author followed by *et al.* and the year (Sparks et al., 1984). When a work has six or more authors, cite the name of the first author followed by *et al.* and the year.

When citing multiple authors in your text, join the names of the last two with *and* (According to Rosen, Wolfe, and Ziff [1988] . . .). In parenthetical documentation, however, use an ampersand to join multiple authors (Rosen, Wolfe, & Ziff, 1988).

Specific parts of a source

When citing a specific part of a source, you should identify that part in your reference. APA documentation includes abbreviations for the words *page* ("p."), *chapter* ("ch."), and *section* ("sec.").

These theories have an interesting history (Lee, 1966, p. 53).

Two or more works within the same parenthetical reference

Identify works by different authors in alphabetical order.

. . . among several studies (Barson & Roth, 1985; Rose, 1987; Tedesco, 1982).

Identify works by the same author in order of date of publication.

. . . among several studies (Weiss & Elliot, 1982, 1984, 1985).

Identify works by the same author that appeared in the same year by designating the first *a*, the second *b*, and so on. (*In press* designates a work about to be published.)

> . . . among several studies (Hossack, 1985a, 1985b, 1985c, in press).

Quotation

For a quotation, a page number appears in addition to the author's name and the year.

> Because of information about Japanese success, the United States has come to realize that "Japanese productivity has successfully challenged, even humiliated, America in world competition" (Bowman, 1984, p. 197).

The page number for a blocked quotation (40 words or more) also appears in parentheses but follows the period that ends the last sentence.

> As Rehder (1983) points out,
> > Here women receive low wages, little job security, and less opportunity for training or educational development . . .
> > (p. 43)

Listing the References

The list of all the sources cited in your paper falls at the end on a new numbered page with the heading *References*.

Items are arranged in alphabetical order, with the author's last name spelled out in full and initials only for the author's first and second names. Next comes the date of publication, title, and, for journal entries, volume number and pages. For books, the date of publication, city of publication, and publisher are included.

Reference List Format

Last name   *initials*   *Underlined title (only first word capitalized)*
↓   ↓   ↓
Morgan, C. T. (1986).   Introduction to psychology. New York: Knopf.
              ↓   ↓   ↓
            Date   *City*   *Publisher*

When determining the order of works in the reference list, keep the following guidelines in mind.

- Single-author entries are arranged before multiple-author entries that begin with the same name.

  Field, S. (1987) . . .
  Field, S., & Levitt, M. P. (1984) . . .

- Entries by the same author are arranged according to the year of publication, starting with the earliest date.

  Ruthenberg, H., & Rubin, R. (1985) . . .
  Ruthenberg, H., & Rubin, R. (1987) . . .

- Entries by the same author and having the same year of publication are arranged alphabetically according to title. They include lower-case letters after the year.

  Wolk, E. M. (1986a). Analysis . . .
  Wolk, E. M. (1986b). Hormonal . . .

Sample Citations—Books

Capitalize only the first word of the title and the first word of the subtitle of books. Be sure to underline the title and to enclose in parentheses the date, volume number, and edition number.

A book with one author

  Maslow, A. H. (1974). <u>Toward a psychology of being</u>. Princeton: Van
      Nostrand.

A book with more than one author

Notice that both authors are cited with last names first.

  Blood, R. O., & Wolf, D. M. (1960). <u>Husbands and wives: The dynamics
      of married living</u>. Glencoe: Free Press.

An edited book

  Lewin, K., Lippitt, R., & White, R. K. (Eds.). (1985). <u>Social
      learning and imitation</u>. New York: Basic Books.

A volume of a multivolume work

> Gibb, C. A. (1969). Leadership. In G. Linzey and E. Aronson (Eds.),
> Handbook of social psychology (Vol. 4, pp. 205-282). Reading,
> MA: Addison-Wesley.

A later edition

> Boshes, L. D., & Gibbs, F. A. (1972). Epilepsy handbook (2nd ed.).
> Springfield, IL: Thomas.

A book with a corporate author

> League of Women Voters of the United States. (1969). Local league
> handbook. Washington, DC: Author.

A book review

Place material that describes the form or content of the reference—review, interview, and so on—within brackets.

> Nagel, J. H. (1970). The consumer view of advertising in America
> [Review of Advertising in America: The consumer view]. Personal
> Psychology, 23, 133-134.

A translated book

> Carpentier, A. (1976). Reasons of state. (F. Partridge, Trans.).
> New York: W. W. Norton.

Sample Citations—Articles

Capitalize only the first word of the title and the first word of the subtitle of articles. Do not underline the article or enclose it in quotation marks. Give the journal title in full; underline the title and capitalize all major words. Underline the volume number and include the issue number in parentheses. Give inclusive page numbers.

An article in a scholarly journal with continuous pagination through an annual volume

> Miller, W. (1969). Violent crimes in city gangs. Journal of Social
> Issues, 27, 581-593.

An article in a scholarly journal that has separate pagination in each issue

> Williams, S., & Cohen, L. R. (1984). Child stress in early learning
> situations. American Psychologist, 21, (10), 1-28.

An encyclopedia article

> Hodge, R. W., & Siegel, P. M. (1968). The measurement of social
> class. In D. L. Sills (Ed.), International encyclopedia of the
> social sciences (Vol. 15, pp. 316-324). New York: Macmillan.

A magazine article

Use *p.* or *pp.* when referring to page numbers in magazines and newspapers, but omit this abbreviation when referring to page numbers in journals.

> Miller, G. A. (1984, November). The test: Alfred Binet's method of
> identifying subnormal children. Science 84, pp. 55-57.

A newspaper article

> Study finds many street people mentally ill. (1984, June). New York
> Times, p. 7.
> Boffy, P. M. (1982, January 24). Security and science collide on data
> flow. New York Times, p. 20.

An article in an edited book

> Tappan, P. W. (1980). Who is a criminal? In M. E. Wolfgang,
> L. Savitz, & N. Johnston (Eds.), The sociology of crime and
> delinquency (pp. 41-48). New York: Wiley.

A government publication

> National Institute of Mental Health. (1985). Television and the
> family: A report on the effect on children of violence and family
> television viewing (DHHS Publication No. ADM 85-1274).
> Washington, DC: U.S. Government Printing Office.

An abstract

```
Pippard, J., & Ellam, L. (1981). Electroconvulsive treatment in
    Great Britain. British Journal of Psychiatry, 139, 563-568.
    (From Psychological Abstracts, 1982, 68, Abstract No. 1567).
```

Sample Citations—Non-print Sources

A film or videotape

```
Kramer, S. (Producer), & Benedek, L. (Director). (1951). Death of a
    salesman [Film]. Columbia.
```

An interview

```
Anderson, A., & Southern, T. (1958). [Interview with Nelson Algren].
    In M. Cowley (Ed.), Writers at work (pp. 231-249). New York:
    Viking.
```

If the interview is not published, it does not appear in "References." Instead, the text of the paper should clarify the interview's nature and date.

SAMPLE PAPERS IN THE SOCIAL SCIENCES

The following student papers—"Student Stress and Attrition" and "Civilian Control of Atomic Energy: Scientists' Bridge into Politics"—illustrate APA format.

SAMPLE SOCIAL SCIENCE PAPER: APA FORMAT

Student Stress
1

Student Stress and Attrition

To: Richard Hanke, Residence Hall Coordinator

From: Gloria E. Medrano, Resident Assistant

Purpose: To present information on stress that would be
         relevant to our Residence Halls Administration

Student Stress
2

*short title and
number on
every page*

Student Stress and Attrition

title repeated

*interesting
statistic for
introduction*

    The National Center for Educational Statistics
predicts an overall decrease of 7.5% in student enrollments
between 1980 and 1988. This statistic translates into a
decrease in undergraduate enrollments for four-year
institutions of approximately 17%. This situation, coupled
with present decreases in federal and state support for
higher education, explains why 60% of the nation's college
presidents agree that enrollment is a major concern (Dusek
and Renteria, 1984).

*author's name
in parentheses
when omitted
from text*

    Ecklund and Henderson (1981), in their national
longitudinal study of the high school class of 1972,
documented how 46% of enrolling college freshmen had at one
point or another dropped out of college. Thirty-four
percent dropped out within their first two years (Ecklund
and Henderson, 1981). The decreasing student populations
and high dropout rates are directly affecting the state of
our educational system. Although there is little that can
be done about the lower numbers of incoming freshmen,
something can be done to lessen the problem of college
attrition.

    The ideal approach to combatting this problem is to
deal with the group of students closest in proximity to the

Student Stress
3

university--the residence hall population. Many of their

reasons for withdrawing from the university are traced to a

fundamental cause: stress. In this case stress is the

psychological phenomenon that contributes to the high   *states thesis*

attrition rates of resident students.

Statement of the Problem

    The on-campus resident student population is very   *distinguishes*
and classifies
different from other groups of individuals. They cannot   *the group to*
be studied
be compared to such groups as non-students, non-commuters,

and commuters. Aside from such student-related stressors

as academics and personal, financial, and emotional

problems, on-campus resident students must also contend

with adjusting to their new environment, living away

from home and in a new community, having a roommate, and

being disturbed by the overall noise level in the

dormitories.

    Bishop and Snyder (1976) noted grades and money as the   *year in*
parentheses —
major pressures that account for the differences between   *author's name*
in text
residents and commuters. Commuters ranked time management

next on their list, and residents listed social pressures

and concerns about their future as their next most prominent

problem. Residents cited peer pressure more often as

sources of stress while commuters were more concerned with

difficulties of scheduling.

Student Stress
4

Background of the Problem

Resident students at the University of Texas at El Paso experience problems which are different and distinct from other major universities. Of the more than 15,000 students attending this university, slightly over 700 live on campus. This is a relatively small percentage compared to the neighboring campus of New Mexico State University, where over 1500 of the 12,000 students live on campus (Hanke, personal communication, December 1984). U.T. El Paso is a commuter campus, which means that between the hours of 1 P.M. and 5 P.M. the campus is virtually deserted. Many other universities, like N.M.S.U., have campus-oriented communities. The students have many activities with which to fill their time. As stated earlier, the social atmosphere is directly related to student stress levels. Many of our on-campus residents are from out of town, with no means of transportation to get them off campus, and there is no immediate community around the campus. They are therefore unable to expand their social outlets. Another factor which relates to UTEP is that many of our residents are freshmen; they are often unfamiliar with many campus activities that would serve to break the monotony of campus living. Because of the low numbers of on-campus residents and the high numbers of commuting students, residents are also limited in terms of the potential number of people they can interact with.

background of the group to be studied

use of comparison and contrast to highlight problem

Student Stress
5

The new system of incorporating athletes into the
regular student housing system has been particularly
traumatic for non-athlete residents. Previously, athletes
were housed in a separate dormitory, Burges Hall; however,
because that hall has fallen into disrepair, the incoming
freshmen football players have been moved into Barry Hall's
third floor. This floor is between two other non-academic
floors. A non-academic floor is one that is not especially
designated for honors students or other students requiring
special study hours. As such, non-academic floors do not
have designated quiet hours or rules and regulations that
foster study and quiet. Aside from the usual noise related
to living in a non-academic dormitory, additional problems,
such as the dropping of weights on the floor and disciplinary
problems related to the rowdiness of athletes in general,
also occur.

Description of the Problem

At the beginning of the fall semester of 1984, Barry
Hall's second floor had twenty-two residents. Three
residents dropped out of school because of personal and
family problems, and two residents moved to other floors
because of a roommate conflict that could not be resolved.
Of the remaining seventeen residents, eleven will be
returning to the University in the spring semester. Five

*generalized
description of
the problem
related to the
specific case*

students are leaving the system to study at a university
closer to home, and one is moving out of the dormitory
into an apartment. Five of the returning students will
move back to Barry Hall's second floor, while six will
be moving to other floors after having been seriously
frustrated by living on a non-academic floor. This
shows the variety of different stressful situations
that can occur on a dormitory floor.

Solutions

Although the dropout rate caused by stress in the
dormitories does not significantly affect the university
because most students are commuters, it is a problem which,
if alleviated, will help to solve the institution's overall
retention problem. At a time when UTEP is concerned with
decreasing enrollments, maintaining enrollments is
important. The implementation of a wide range of
educational and social programming within the residence
halls, strengthening the programs of recruitment,
admissions, counseling services, financial aid, career
planning and placement, and health services will also
contribute to decreased stress and improved retention.

It is imperative that those individuals who have the
closest contact with the resident students--their resident
assistants--be trained in handling stress. Additionally,
they must be introduced thoroughly to the services

available on campus. Resident assistants can work closely
with, for instance, the New Students Relations office to
point out incoming freshmen who might be prone to drop out.
Resident assistants should also be involved in the working
of the freshmen orientation program and in other programs
which can help students. These programs and departments
include Financial Aid, The Career Information Center,
Counseling Services, the Health Center, Placement Services,
Student Association, and Study Skills.

Resident assistants should pay particular attention
to their residents and watch for signs which warn them if
students are having stress-related problems. If a resident
assistant suspects that a resident is having a special
problem, the resident can be referred to an appropriate
program or department for help.

With proper training resident advisors can take the
necessary steps to control the 50% attrition rates among
on-campus resident students.

References

Bishop, J. B. and Snyder, G. S. (1976). Commuters and
    residents: Pressures, helps and psychological
    services. Journal of College Student Personnel,
    17, 232-235.

Ecklund, B. K. & Henderson, L. B. (1981). Longitudinal
    study of the high school class of 1972. Washington,
    DC: National Institute of Education. (Eric Document
    Reproduction No. ED 311-222).

Dusek, R. & Renteria, R. (1984, December 13). Plan slashes
    UTEP budget by 28%. El Paso Times, p. A1.

Hanke, R. (1984, December). [Interview with Gloria
    Medrano].

SAMPLE SOCIAL SCIENCE PAPER—APA FORMAT

Civilian Control of Atomic Energy:

Scientists' Bridge into Politics

by

Jeanne Parker

Political Science 102

Dr. Richard Gregory

March 8, 1989

Outline

Thesis: The atomic bomb motivated scientists to enter
post-World War II politics.

I.   End-of-war attitudes of scientists toward control of
     atomic energy

     A. Franck Report: international agreement

     B. Einstein and others: world government

II. Postwar activities of scientists

     A. Ability to influence public policy

         1. Had greatest knowledge of bomb

         2. Enjoyed great public prestige

     B. Drawbacks of influencing public policy

         1. Reluctant to get involved in politics

         2. Temperamentally unsuited for role as lobbyists

III. The May-Johnson Bill

     A. Provisions of the bill

         1. Military control

         2. Nine-member commission

     B. Objections of scientists

         1. Wanted to resume prewar lives

         2. Wanted freedom from regimentation

         3. Opposed military secrecy

         4. Feared limits on equipment and personnel

IV. Actions of scientists against military control

     A. Opposed May-Johnson Bill

Civilian Control
2

       1. Organized the Federation of American Scientists

       2. Lobbied despite reluctance

       3. Convinced Truman to withdraw support

  B. Supported McMahon Bill

  C. Opposed Vandenberg Amendment

V. Conclusion

  A. Scientists entered politics

       1. Learned to influence public opinion

       2. Learned to influence government policy

  B. Scientists helped determine the future of atomic
     energy

Civilian Control of Atomic Energy:

Scientists' Bridge into Politics

In 1939 a group of physicists who had fled to the
United States from Hitler's Germany persuaded President
Roosevelt to begin work on an atomic bomb. Six years later,
on August 6, 1945, the United States dropped an atomic bomb
on the Japanese city of Hiroshima and a second bomb on
Nagasaki three days later. The world was stunned, mainly
because no one, except for a handful of political and
military leaders, knew we were working on an atomic weapon.
Also, its power surprised everyone, even the scientists who
built it. For most of these scientists, however, the
greatest shock came with the realization that in the new
atomic age which their efforts had created, they could no
longer remain aloof from politics. Having urged the
creation of the atomic bomb, many scientists felt obligated
to take steps to ensure that the governments of the world
used atomic energy for the good of mankind, not for its
destruction. Thus, in the words of Hans Bethe (Smith,
1971), a leading physicist, the atomic bomb "changed
everything; it took scientists into politics."

Even before the end of the war, many scientists
foresaw the need for some form of governmental control over
atomic energy. As scientists, they knew that the atom was

Civilian Control
4

potentially a source of enormous, even unlimited power. Working on the Manhattan Project, as the American effort to build the atomic bomb was called, they were attempting to liberate this power for use in a weapon. They realized, however, that because the basic physics of nuclear reactions, the kind that caused an atomic bomb to explode, was widely known, the American monopoly on nuclear weapons would not last long (Jungk, 1958). Once another nation acquired an atomic bomb, so the scientists reasoned, the world would be locked into a spiraling arms race.

Most scientists concluded that the only way to prevent this was some form of international control. Probably the most important statement of these concerns is the Franck Report, written by a committee of scientists at the University of Chicago in June 1945. A month before the first atomic bomb was tested, these scientists peered ahead into a future filled with dangers. Their immediate concern was to argue that the bomb should not be used against the Japanese. Like many other scientists, the Franck Committee saw no alternative to international control of nuclear weapons. The problem, however, was whether using the bomb against the Japanese would make it virtually impossible to get other nations to join us in some form of international agreement. "It may be very difficult to persuade the world that a nation which was capable of secretly preparing and suddenly releasing . . . [the atomic bomb] is to be trusted in its proclaimed desire of having such weapons abolished by international agreement" (Smith, 1970, p. 377).

Some scientists went even further. Like the scientists who wrote the Franck Report, they foresaw that an arms race was inevitable unless the nations of the world agreed not to build atomic bombs. But they did not believe that a mere agreement was sufficient to eliminate the threat. A few of them argued that a world filled with atomic weapons was so dangerous that the nations of the world would have to surrender their sovereignty to some form of international government if humankind were to avoid destroying itself. Probably the best-known advocate of world government was Albert Einstein, who, in November 1945, published an article arguing that a world government was necessary. The alternative, he declared, was nuclear war some time in the future:

> Do I fear the tyranny of a world government? Of course I do. But I fear still more the coming of another war. Any government is certain to be evil to some extent. But a world government is preferable to the far greater evil of wars, particularly when viewed in the context of the intensified destructiveness of war. If such a world government is not established by a process

Civilian Control
6

of agreement among nations, I believe it will
come anyway, and in a much more dangerous form;
for war or wars can only result in one power
being supreme and dominating the rest of the
world by its overwhelming military supremacy
(p. 349).

In other words, the nations of the world could either join
together now in a world government or wait for one nation to
emerge victorious over the rest of the world after a nuclear
holocaust.

Many atomic scientists, then, saw no alternative to
some form of international control, although few went so far
as to advocate world government. The enormity of their
discoveries forced them to conclusions like these. However,
the failure of their efforts to influence the decision to use
the bomb against Japan convinced many scientists that they
would have to organize in order to lobby more effectively for
their views (Jungk, 1958, pp. 221-23).

After the war, therefore, scientists at the major sites
of the Manhattan Project--Los Alamos, New Mexico; Oak Ridge,
Tennessee; and Hanford, Washington--organized into groups
whose purpose was "to promote the attainment and use of
scientific and technological advances in the best interests
of humanity" (Strickland, 1968, p. 38). In the closing
months of 1945, many scientists felt they were in a unique

position to influence the outcome of contemporary debates over control of the atom. First, unlike the general public and nearly all government and military leaders, scientists at Los Alamos, Oak Ridge, Hanford, and especially at the University of Chicago had had a long time to contemplate the consequence of their discoveries since they were virtually the only ones who knew anything at all about the bomb until August 6, 1945 (Jungk, 1958, pp. 115-17). Second, after the war they enjoyed great public prestige. Once the secret was out, the popular press was filled with accounts of the Manhattan Project, its scientific director, J. Robert Oppenheimer, and the secret cities of Los Alamos and Oak Ridge that the army had erected for the purpose of creating the bomb. Writing in 1945, Daniel Lang (p. 58) noted that "atom" had become "a magic word in Washington" and that the atomic scientists, the only ones who fully understood its meaning, were looked upon as "glamour boys." One scientist observed that before the war, scientists were seen by the public as being naive and detached from the world. But after the bomb, they were seen as "the ultimate authorities on all possible subjects, from nylon stockings to the best form of international organization" (Jungk, 1958).

As the tone of these comments suggests, the scientists themselves were often unsure of how to use their new prestige. It was one thing to know what, in their

judgment, the government ought to do; it was quite
another matter to get the government to do it. First, they
had to overcome the traditional reluctance of scientists to
involve themselves with politics. According to Daniel S.
Greenberg (1971), the "war-born relationship" between
American science and politics seemed to reverse nearly two
centuries of "mutual aloofness between the federal
government and the most influential and creative segments
of the scientific community." Second, most scientists were
temperamentally unsuited to their new roles as lobbyists.
Daniel Lang (1959, p. 60) makes this point:

> They were accustomed to objectivity. An
> experiment worked or it didn't, data were
> correct or incorrect; there was no middle
> ground. They found it difficult to adjust
> themselves to the give-and-take way of getting
> things done in Washington, and they were unable
> to understand why everybody couldn't see at
> once how right they were.

Finally, many leading scientists cautioned their colleagues
to refrain from any sort of public comment or political
action which might jeopardize the chances of getting some
form of control. For example, Robert Oppenheimer warned the
Association of Los Alamos Scientists that one of their
proposed public statements might be calamitous to a new bill

being written by the Truman administration
(Strickland, 1968).

But that new bill, the May-Johnson Bill, quickly
forced the scientists to overcome all of their prejudices
against political involvement and doubts about their
political effectiveness. The May-Johnson Bill was the
first legislation proposed to deal with the domestic
control of atomic energy. Although the atomic scientists
still hoped that the administration would propose a plan for
international control, they were greatly upset by several
provisions of this bill, notably its proposal to continue
military control over atomic research. Thus most scientists
quickly switched their effort from proposing different
schemes for international control of atomic energy to
blocking the passage of the May-Johnson Bill.

The May-Johnson Bill proposed a part-time commission
of nine members selected by the president with the Senate's
consent. These nine members would then choose their own
administrator and deputy administrator, and any of these
positions could be held by military officers. The
commission would be given broad power over nearly all
aspects of atomic energy, including scientific research
(Hewlett and Anderson, 1962).

The scientists opposed continued military control
over atomic research for a number of reasons. After the

hard years at Los Alamos and other project sites, they were looking forward to freedom from military discipline. Even before the bill was proposed, the scientists had had enough of the military involvement in their lives. Although the war was finally over, they soon discovered that "everything was to go on as before" (Jungk, 1958, p. 227). These scientists wanted to go back to their research, their universities, and their homes to live as they had before the war. Moreover, their experiences on the Manhattan Project convinced some of them that their freedom to work on new ideas would be curtailed by continued military control. Testifying for the May-Johnson Bill, J. Robert Oppenheimer admitted that "scientists are not used to being controlled; they are not used to regimentation, and there are good reasons why they should be averse to it, because it is in the nature of science that the individual is to be given a certain amount of freedom to think, and to carry on the best he knows how" (United States, 1946, p. 28). Oppenheimer spoke from experience; as director of the Los Alamos laboratory, he had successfully resisted pressure from General Leslie Groves, military head of the Manhattan Project, to enlist project scientists into the army (Goodchild, 1981).

In addition, they felt the need to inform the public about the facts of this new and mysterious weapon. They

soon found that the strict secrecy regulations were
also "to go on as before" and under the May-Johnson Bill
would continue indefinitely with regard to foreign policy.
There was much concern by the administration that the
"secret" of the atom bomb would escape to other
countries. This position infuriated the scientists
because they argued that there was no secret. They felt
that the only secret was the procedure, but within a few
years any country could experiment, as the United States
had, and discover that very same secret. The scientists
also felt that secrecy would hurt the United States' atomic
project. Robert Cushman (1947) summed up the scientists'
views on this subject when he said, "It would be calamitous
to shut off the broad and free discussion of the basic
points involved, since it is only by such free discussion
that we can hope to increase our wisdom and inform public
opinion with respect to the vital questions of policy which
must be faced" (p. 58).

The last reason the scientists disapproved of
military control of atomic energy was that they had reason
to fear that the military would restrict the equipment and
personnel they needed. These scientists remembered too
well what it was like during the war. They used as an
example to support their disapproval an event that occurred
at the Metallurgical Lab. A request was sent in for linoleum

flooring to go under a sensitive piece of equipment
being used, but the army did not accept it at first, because
they did not see the necessity of it. One man involved
said, "You had to lose your temper--they wouldn't take your
word for it otherwise" (Strickland, 1968). Furthermore,
the army's detailed examinations and investigations might
reject a fully qualified scientist who would aid the
project. They felt that this would inhibit the natural
growth of knowledge acquired on atomic energy.

The majority of scientists, then, opposed the
May-Johnson Bill and supported the concept of civilian
control. In an effort to defeat the bill, they began
organizing themselves into the Federation of Atomic
Scientists (later to be changed to the Federation of
American Scientists) (Lang, 1959). Their strategy for
action was to change public opinion and to lobby directly in
Washington. At first the scientists were somewhat reluctant
to lobby because they felt that "science should not be
dragged through the political arena" (Hewlett and Anderson,
1962, p. 448). But they still saw the necessity of action.
Their attitude began to change as they got more involved
with the legislators and officials. Everyone in Washington
and all over the country was hungry for information on
atomic energy, so the scientists had to force no one to
listen to their views.

Their lobbying efforts, although time-consuming, were successful; at the beginning of December, President Truman withdrew his support of the May-Johnson Bill, and its argument collapsed under the pressure exerted. The scientists had good reason for rejoicing, but their work was not yet finished. Although the threat of May-Johnson had been eliminated, there was no acceptable bill to take its place. On December 20, such a bill, the McMahon Bill, was introduced (Hewlett and Anderson, 1962, pp. 439-43).

Just as the May-Johnson Bill proposed military control of atomic energy, the new McMahon Bill proposed civilian control. It created a five-member, full-time, civilian commission that would report directly to the president. It would have broad powers to supervise and regulate atomic research and fissionable materials and to study social and health effects of experiments and uses (Hewlett and Anderson, 1962, pp. 714-22). Because of its emphasis on civilian control, the scientists felt that the McMahon Bill was an acceptable alternative to the May-Johnson Bill. The scientists openly supported the McMahon Bill, using the techniques they had used to attack the May-Johnson Bill.

Things were beginning to look optimistic for passage of the bill until, during the McMahon hearings, from January 22 to April 8, 1946, the Vandenberg Amendment was proposed.

This amendment suggested that a military liaison, who
would have some influence on all the decisions dealing with
national security, be attached to the commission. The
amendment infuriated the scientists because they felt that
it was "a clear declaration to the world that the people of
the United States will put their faith only in military
might" ("The Army," 1946). They also feared that the
liaison would take away the powers of the commission but
leave the responsibilities. Opposition to this amendment
renewed the protests of the scientists and the public shown
during the fall of 1945, and it was through this intensity
of action that the Vandenberg Amendment was defeated. An
article in the New Republic ("Civilian," 1946) credited the
scientists' lobby with the victory, saying that McMahon,
the scientists, and public opinion caused Vandenberg and his
supporters on the Senate Committee to back down. On June 1,
1946, the McMahon Bill was passed by the Senate and was soon
to be passed by the Senate-House Conference Committee. It
was signed by the president on August 1 and became law as
the Atomic Energy Act of 1946 ("The Army," 1946).

By taking an active part in politics, the scientists
had learned that they could affect public opinion and
influence government policy. Their success indicates they
learned this lesson well: during the last few weeks of the
Senate committee investigations, 70,972 letters were

received, with 24,851 expressing views opposing the
Vandenberg Amendment, 35,000 opposing the May-Johnson Bill,
and only a dozen opposing the McMahon Bill. Petitions were
sent in with thousands of signatures. If the scientists had
not felt the need to actively oppose the May-Johnson Bill
and support the McMahon Bill and the decision had gone the
other way, it would have meant a change in national policy
with respect to atomic energy. However, these two bills are
important not only in themselves but also because the
controversy they engendered made scientists, politicians,
and the general public aware of the perplexities and
problems of life in the Nuclear Age.

References

The army and the atom. (1946, May 23). Nation, pp. 333-34.

Civilian atomic control. (1946, April 15). New Republic,
     p. 494.

Cushman, E. (1947, January). Civil liberties in the atomic
     age: Threat of military control. Annals of the
     American Academy of Political and Social Sciences,
     249, 54-60.

Einstein, A. (1968). Atomic war or peace. In O. Nathan and
     H. Norden (Eds.), Einstein on peace. (pp. 340-355).
     New York: Schocken.

Goodchild, P. (1981). J. Robert Oppenheimer: Shatterer of
     worlds. Boston: Houghton.

Greenberg, S. (1971). The politics of pure science.
     (1967). New York: New American.

Hewlett, R. G. and E. Anderson, Jr. (1962). The new world,
     1939-46. Vol. 1 of A history of the United States
     Atomic Energy Commission. 5 vols. University Park,
     Pa.: Pennsylvania State University Press.

Jungk, R. (1958). Brighter than a thousand suns: A
     personal history of the atomic scientists. Trans.
     James Cleugh. New York: Harcourt.

Lang, D. (1959). From Hiroshima to the moon: Chronicles of
     life in the atomic age. New York: Simon.

106 WRITING IN THE SOCIAL SCIENCES

70 thousand letters back the McMahon bill. (1946,

April 15). Bulletin of the Atomic Scientists, p. 6.

Smith, A. (1971). Los Alamos: Focus of an age. In R. S.

Lewis and J. Wilson (Eds.), Alamogordo plus

twenty-five years. New York: Viking.

Smith, A. K. (1970). A peril and a hope: The scientists'

movement in America, 1945-47. (1965). Cambridge,

Mass.: MIT Press.

Strickland, D. A. (1968). Scientists in politics: The

atomic scientists' movement, 1945-48. Lafayette,

Ind.: Purdue Research Foundation.

United States Department of State. (1946). International

control of atomic energy: Growth of a policy.

Washington, DC: U.S. Government Printing Office.

WRITING IN THE SCIENCES

Science writing consists largely of empirical reporting and writing to meet pragmatic ends such as providing information on how to do something or writing a lab report on a procedure that can be replicated. Most methods of preparing protocols, reports, and literature reviews are common to other subjects. Although science writing may be persuasive, as in a paper arguing that computerized heat treatments are a superior method of treating metals, it is often expository, concerned with accurately reporting observations and experimental data.

RESEARCH SOURCES

The methods of data collection in the sciences frequently entail observation and experimental research. Most results are tabulated and presented graphically. However, literature searches are often carried out in the library.

Specialized Library Sources

The *Science Citation Index* is one of the most widely used indexes in the sciences. Scientists are particularly interested in the number of times and the variety of sources in which an author is cited and therefore use citation indexes frequently. The following specific sources are just some of those available to the sciences.

> **General Science**
> Applied Science and Technology Index
> CRC Handbook of Chemistry and Physics (and other titles in the CRC series of handbooks)
> General Science Index
> McGraw-Hill Encyclopedia of Science and Technology
> Science Citation Index
> **Chemistry**
> Analytical Abstracts
> Chemical Abstracts
> Encyclopedia of Chemistry
> Kirk-Othmer Encyclopedia of Chemical Technology

Engineering
Engineering Encyclopedia
Engineering Index
Environment Index
Government Reports Announcements (NTIS)
HRIS Abstracts (Highway Engineering)

Geology
Abstracts of North American Geology
Annotated Bibliography of Economic Geology
Bibliography and Index of Geology
Bibliography of North American Geology
GeoAbstracts (Geographical Abstracts)
Publications of the USGS
Selected Water Resources Abstracts

Life Sciences
Biological Abstracts
Biological and Agricultural Index
Encyclopedia of Bioethics
Encyclopedia of the Biological Sciences
Index Medicus

Mathematics
Index to Mathematical Papers
Mathematical Reviews
Universal Encyclopedia of Mathematics

Physics
Astronomy and Astrophysics Abstracts
Encyclopedia of Physics
Physics Abstracts
Solid State Abstracts Journal

Specialized Databases for Computer Searches

As with other disciplines, many print indexes are also available on-line. Helpful databases for research in the sciences include *BIOSIS Previews, CASearch, SCISEARCH, Agvicola, CAB Abstracts, Compendex, NTIS, Inspec, MEDLINE, MATHSCI,* and *Life Sciences Collection.*

Non-Library Sources

As stated earlier, much of the research in the sciences is conducted in the laboratory or in the field. Non-library sources in the sciences vary greatly because of the many subjects that make up the sciences. In agronomy, for example, you might need to collect soil samples; in toxicology, you might want to test air or water quality. In marine biology, you might conduct research in a particular aquatic environment, while in chemistry you might collect blood samples.

ASSIGNMENTS IN THE SCIENCES

Many writing assignments in a science class are similar to those assigned in the other disciplines; for instance, they include annotated bibliographies (see "Writing in the Humanities") and proposals (see "Writing in the Social Sciences"). Two additional assignments common in (but not limited to) science disciplines are the abstract, the literature survey, and the laboratory report.

Abstracts

Many scientific indexes provide abstracts of articles so that researchers may know whether an article is of specific use to them. Most scientific articles provide an abstract at the beginning of the article. Such an abstract serves as a road map or guide for readers. An *indicative abstract* merely indicates what the content of an article is. It helps readers decide whether they want to read the article in full or whether the contents of the article are of use to them. An *informative abstract* is detailed enough so that readers can obtain essential information without reading the article itself. Interpretation and criticism are usually not included in an abstract.

In writing an abstract follow the format of the article. State the purpose, method of research, results, and conclusion in the order in which they occur in the article or paper, but include essential information only. An abstract should contain about 200–500 words. Avoid quoting from the article or repeating the title. An abstract should also provide clear information for a wide audience; therefore, avoid much technical vocabulary. Indicative abstracts are used in indexes, card catalogs, and proposals. Informative abstracts are usually included in annotated bibliographies for specialized purposes and summarized in literature survey sections. An annotated bibliography is made up of short indicative abstracts that follow each complete citation in a bibliography.

Literature Surveys

Literature surveys are common to the social sciences—psychology, sociology, political science—and to the sciences. They are usually used in preparing project proposals or as precursors to arguments in a paper in which you might try to prove the uniqueness of your experimental method or your argument. Unlike an abstract which simply gives the necessary information, a literature survey can be argumentative. A literature survey also does much comparison and contrast of the articles which the researcher has read. Here is a sample of a literature survey from a paper written for a biology course in parasitology.

Ultrastructural studies of micro- and macrogametes have included relatively few of the numerous Eimerian species. Major early studies include the following (hosts are listed in parentheses): micro- and macrogametes of E. perforans (rabbits), E. stiedae (rabbits), E. bovis (cattle), and E. auburnensis (cattle) (Hammond et al., 1967; Scholtyseck et al., 1966), macrogametogenesis in E. Magna (rabbits) and E. intestinalis (rabbits) (Kheysin, 1965), macrogametogony of E. tenella (chickens) (McLaren, 1969), and the microgametocytes and macrogametes of E. neischulzi (rats) (Colley, 1967). More recent investigations have included macrogametogony of E. acervulina (chickens) (Pitillo and Ball, 1984).

There is little knowledge concerning the nutrient requirements of the Eimeria, but their parasitic nature is evidence for dependency on host nutrients. Warren (1969) utilized diet deficiency techniques to study the effect of various vitamins or growth factors on the course of E. tenella and E. acervulina infections in chickens. Deficiency in biotin led to a 90% reduction in oocyst production. Biotin, the essential cofactor in biosynthesis of fatty acids and fatty alcohols was found to be necessary for schizogony and gametogony in both parasites. Charney et al. (1971) found that a fatty acid deficient diet reduced the amount of lesions and mortality caused by E. tenella and E. mivati infections in chickens. When corn oil supplement was added the severity of the infection resumed, whereas hydrogenated coconut oil supplement did not counteract the deficiency. These results indicate that coccidia are unable to metabolize some of the essential unsaturated fatty acids. The localization of electron-dense ferritin-biotin complex in intravacuolar tubules would support the hypothesis that they are used for nutrient transport and that biotin is required.

Such a literature survey is usually appropriate only for an audience familiar with the field.

Laboratory Reports

A lab report is perhaps the most common assignment for students taking courses in the sciences. It is divided into sections that generally conform to the specifications for a science paper outlined below. Not every section described in this format will be necessary for every experiment. Some experiments may even call for additional components, such as abstracts or references. In addition, a lab experiment will often include tables, charts, graphs, and illustrations. Much of the time the exact format of a student lab report is defined by the lab manual being used in a specific course.

In general, a lab report is a process description. For this reason, learning to explain a process clearly and completely, with its steps in exact chronological order, and to illustrate the purpose of each step are essential skills for students writing in the sciences. Process description, however, is not confined to describing the steps taken in the lab. The methods and materials section of a lab report also relies on process description, providing clear descriptions of the equipment used in an experiment and explaining its function (unless you can assume that it will be familiar to science students). For instance, in a lab report you must not only describe how you set up a spirit level but also explain the function of the specific tools you used. For example, you might parenthetically define the tools in this manner: "a hand level (a small device which allows the person looking through it to locate points at the same elevation level as the device) and a Philadelphia rod (a graduated leveling rod with a movable marker)."

CONVENTIONS OF STYLE AND FORMAT

In writing your lab report or scientific paper, use the passive voice to emphasize tasks rather than the person performing them. Avoid using the second person—that is, avoid giving instructions and directions. It is acceptable to use the first person when writing about your own experiment. Direct quotations are not often used in scientific papers.

Think of the purpose of your writing as providing information for other scientists. This means that you should attempt to clarify your language so that scientists in different science disciplines can understand what you have written. Over-reliance on technical jargon can hamper the clarity and communicability of your paper.

Typically the science paper is divided into four main sections: introduction, methods, results, and conclusion. These sections are often preceded by a title page and an abstract.

- The **introduction** should include the topic, an indication of the scope of the present paper or experiment, a statement of the purpose of the investigation, and a brief mention of the general method of the investigation, perhaps explaining why this method was used over an alternative method. The introduction may sometimes include a literature survey.

- The **methods and materials** section lists equipment used and describes chronologically the steps of the experiment. It is a straightforward description of how you carried out your investigation. Often included in this discussion is a description of the equipment, the materials, and the method of collecting data.
- The **results section** presents a clear description of the data that you have collected. Quite often this section contains a graph of the data and a verbal statement of the results. Calculations, printouts, and other raw data are frequently presented in appendices. Note that this section should not present any conclusions.
- The **conclusion** presents a discussion of the results. It explains the importance of your results and may compare them with those discussed in the literature survey. In addition, you may justify your observations according to theory and explain any problems encountered in carrying out your experiment.

Tables and illustrations are an important part of most scientific papers. Some tables, illustrations, and graphs present results, while others may describe methods and materials. Tables should be placed as close to the discussion of them as possible. Even so, any type of illustration or diagram must be numbered and labeled clearly (Figure 1 or Figure 2) so that you can refer to it in your text.

DOCUMENTATION FORMATS

Documentation style varies from one scientific discipline to another; even within each discipline, style may vary from one journal to another. For this reason, you should ask your instructor what documentation format is required. Most disciplines in the sciences use the formats prescribed by their professional societies. For instance, electrical engineers use the format of the Institute for Electronics and Electrical Engineers, chemists use the format of the American Chemical Society, physicists use the format of the American Institute of Physics, mathematicians use the format of the American Mathematical Society, and biologists use the Council of Biology Editors' (CBE) Style Sheet.

THE CBE FORMAT*

CBE format is the documentation format recommended by the Council of Biology Editors and distributed by the American Institute of Biological Sciences. It is used

---

*CBE documentation format follows the guidelines set in the CBE *Style Manual*. 5th ed. Bethesda: Council of Biology Editors, 1983.

by authors, editors, and publishers in biology, botany, zoology, physiology, anatomy, and genetics. The number-reference format recommended by the *CBE Style Manual* is similar to the formats used in the applied and medical sciences. Numbers inserted parenthetically in the text correspond to a reference list at the end of the paper. Works are arranged in the order in which they are mentioned in the text and then numbered consecutively. When the list of references is typed, all lines begin at the left margin.

- **In the paper**

  One study (1) has demonstrated the effect of low dissolved oxygen. Cell walls of. . . .

- **In the reference list**

  Name   *Initials*   *Title not underlined (only first word capitalized)*
    ↓   ↓   ↓
  1. White, R. P. An introduction to biochemistry. Philadelphia:
  W. B. Saunders; 1974.   ↑
           ↑   ↑
       Publisher   *Date*   *City*

Sample Citations—Books

For book entries, list the author(s), the title (with only the first word capitalized), the city of publication followed by a colon, the name of the publisher followed by a semicolon, and the year followed by a period. Do not underline book titles.

A book with one author

  1. Rathmil, P. D. The synthesis of milk and related products. Madison, WI: Hugo Summer; 1985.

A book with more than one author

  2. Krause, K. F.; Paterson, M. K., Jr. Tissue culture: methods and application. New York: Academic Press; 1973.

An edited book

  3. Marzacco, M. P., A survey of biochemistry. New York: R. R. Bowker Co.; 1985.

A specific edition of a book

```
4.  Baldwin, L. D.; Rigby, C. V. A study of animal virology. 2nd
    ed. New York: John Wiley & Sons; 1984:121-133.
```

Sample Citations—Articles

For journal articles list the author(s), the title of the article (with only the first word capitalized), the title of the journal (capitalized, not underlined), the volume number followed by a colon, the inclusive page numbers of the article, and the year followed by a period.

An article in a scholarly journal with continuous pagination in each issue

```
1.  Bensley, L. Profiling women physicians. Medica 1:140-145; 1985.
```

An article in a scholarly journal that has separate pagination in each issue

```
2.  Wilen, W. W. The biological clock of insects. Sci. Amer.
    234(2):114-121; 1976.
```

An article with a subtitle

```
3.  Schindler, A.; Donner, K. B. On DNA: the evolution of an amino
    acid sequence. J. Mol. Evol. 8:94-101; 1980.
```

An article with no author

```
4.  Anonymous. Developments in microbiology. Int. J. Microbiol.
    6:234-248; 1987.
```

An article with discontinuous pages

```
5.  Williams, S.; Heller, G. A. Special dietary foods and their
    importance for diabetics. Food Prod. Dev. 44:54-62, 68-73; 1984.
```

Other Science Formats

In preparing your paper remember that although the *Council of Biology Editors'* style sheet governs the overall presentation of papers in biology, *The Journal of Immunology* might have a different format from the The Journal of Parasitology. (The CBE Style Manual lists the different journals that use their own style formats.) Your teacher may ask you to prepare your paper according to the style sheet of the journal to which you wish to submit your work. Although publication may seem a remote possibility to you, the fact that various groups use different formats underscores the fact that the readers in those groups use that format as a language for understanding one another. Browsing in the disciplinary area will make you familiar with the differences among each discipline.

Each professional society also prescribes the formats of charts and the way they are to be referred to in the text. Therefore, it is difficult to use one format for all the sciences. Also important to learn are the various abbreviations with which journals are referred to in the reference sections of science papers. For example: The American Journal of Physiology is abbreviated Amer. J. Physiol. and The Journal of Physiological Chemistry is abbreviated J. of Physiol. Chemistry. Note that in the CBE reference list, the abbreviated forms of journal titles are not underlined. Since elaborate rules exist for creating abbreviations—for instance, you should always add a consonant to your abbreviation (Biol., not bio., for biology)—consult the appropriate style sheet if you have questions.

Journals in the sciences use a variation of either the number–reference system or the parenthetical notation of author-date system. However it is imperative that the citations be consistent with the practice of the journal, for this means that they are consistent with the practice of researchers in the field.

1. The *author-date system* requires you to note the authors' last names and date of publication of the works you cite in your paper. ["Smith and Jones (1980) conducted the following research. . . ."]. These citations are keyed to an alphabetical list of references at the end of the paper. (See the sample paper on pages 139–143 for an example of the author-date format.)

2. The *number–reference system* requires you to list all the works used in alphabetical order (sometimes in order of use) and assign each a number. Then, whenever you cite the author, you provide the number of that specific reference. Such a method can be fairly cumbersome to readers who must turn back to the reference list to find out the full citation. With parenthetical references, the name of the person or source being cited is readily available.

Here is a list of some common documentation styles used by science disciplines.

American Institute of Physics. *Style Manual*. New York: American Institute of Physics, 1967.

American Mathematical Society. *Manual for Authors of Mathematical Papers* 6th ed. Providence, R.I.: The Society, 1979.

American Medical Association-Scientific Publications Division. *Stylebook: Editorial Manual*. Littleton, Mass: Publishing Sciences Group, 1976.

Conference of Biological Editors. *Style Manual for Biological Journals* 2nd ed. Washington, D.C.: American Institute of Biological Sciences, 1964.

Council of Biological Editors. *Style Manual: A Guide for Authors, Editors and Publishers in the Biological Sciences* 5th ed. Arlington, Va: American Institute of Biology Editors, 1983.

Dodd, Janet S., ed. *The ACS Style Manual.* Washington, D.C.: American Chemical Society, 1986.

SAMPLE PAPERS IN THE SCIENCES

The following student papers—"Shell Selection by Intertidal Hermit Crabs in the Gulf of California" and "The Study of Fossil Flowers"—illustrate the CBE format and author–date formats.

SAMPLE SCIENCE PAPER: CBE FORMAT

Shell Selection by Intertidal Hermit Crabs

in the Gulf of California

Russell R. Broaddus, Marcia L. Hansel, and Jennifer Richer

Correspondence: Jennifer Richer

Department of Biological Sciences

The University of Texas at El Paso

El Paso, Texas 79968

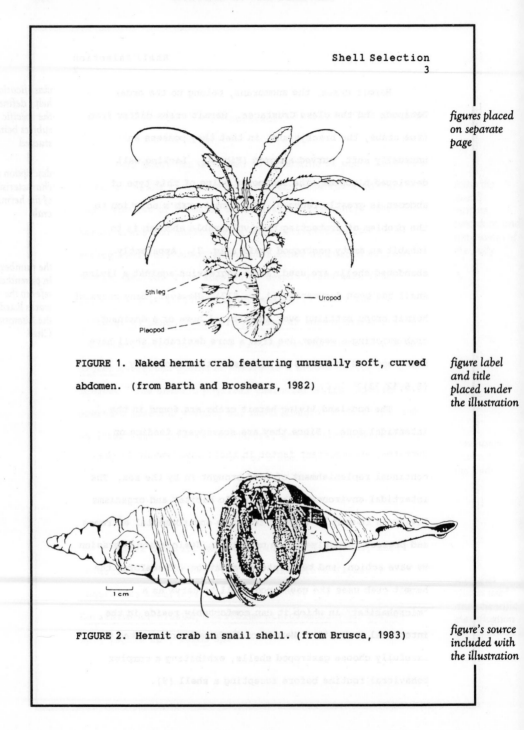

FIGURE 1. Naked hermit crab featuring unusually soft, curved abdomen. (from Barth and Broshears, 1982)

FIGURE 2. Hermit crab in snail shell. (from Brusca, 1983)

figures placed on separate page

figure label and title placed under the illustration

figure's source included with the illustration

Shell Selection
4

Researchers have discovered that hermit crabs are found more frequently in some species of shell than in others (2,4,8,11,12,13). Therefore, it is apparent that hermit crab distribution in gastropod shells is not random. The important question lies in whether or not actual preference is occurring whereby specific species of hermit crabs select particular species of gastropod shells, or if they are simply choosing the most abundant species of shell available. The present study was designed to examine shell selection by hermit crabs in two different intertidal environments on the coast of the Gulf of California in Puerto Peñasco, Sonora, Mexico, and to determine if the distribution of the various species of hermit crabs in the indigenous species of gastropod shells was indicative of actual shell preferences or if shell selection was based on shell availability alone.

refers to several sources at once, indicating that several researchers have made similar observations

statement of purpose

Materials and Methods

Hermit crabs were collected at two ecologically different sites in Puerto Peñasco, Sonora, Mexico. One site was near the Centro de Estudios de Desiertos y Oceanos (CEDO) and the other, approximately 2 miles away, was near the Garcia House. The collection site near CEDO consisted of Coquina limestone reef flats with depressions and very few boulders. These reef flats were interspersed with large sand

details and description of the site of the study

bars. The continental shelf gradually declined, resulting
in shallow tide pools with an unstable environment due to
fluctuating water temperature and increased tide
disturbance. The Garcia House site, on the other hand,
consisted of a large sandbar covered with boulders,
followed by a large Coquina limestone reef to the seaward.
Furthermore, the continental shelf sharply declined,
forming deeper tide pools and providing a more stable
environment with relatively constant water temperatures
and less tidal disturbance.

Morning collections were made at CEDO during low tide
while collections at the Garcia House were made during the
evening low tide. A transect line was stretched from the
shore to the low tide point. The radius of collection
ranged from 1-6 m along the transect, depending on how far
out the tide was and the abundance of shells in the area.
The transect line was moved for each collection so as not to
deplete the hermit crab population.

Both the inhabited and the empty snail shells were
collected in buckets of sea water and transported to the
CEDO lab for crab and snail shell identification. The crabs
were identified in the shell whenever possible, but if a
crab could not be seen, the shell was held directly up to a
dissecting microscope light, allowing one to see through
the shell to determine if a crab inhabited it. If a crab was

*description of
procedure used
to collect
specimens*

Shell Selection
6

present inside the shell, the shell was placed on a hot

plate, which stimulated the crab to leave its shell.

Identification of the hermit crabs and snail shells was

according to Brusca (3, p. 280). As soon as identification

was completed, the hermits and the shells were returned to

their original site in the sea.

page number included with reference number

Results

Five species of hermit crabs were found predominantly

in seven different species of snail shells collected from

CEDO and the Garcia House. Table I shows that Clibanarius

digueti and Pagurristes anahuacus were the most populous

hermit crabs at CEDO and the Garcia House, respectively.

Cerithium stercusmuscarum snail shells were by far the most

abundant at CEDO, whereas Turbo and Morula shells were the

most abundant at the Garcia House (Table II). From these

tables, it can be seen that Cerithium maculosum and Morula

shells were rarely inhabited at CEDO, even though both

shells were common at this location.

reference to tables provides scientists the chance to examine the evidence

lists the results briefly; the discussion section analyzes the results

At CEDO, Pagarus lepidus, P. anahuacus, and

Clibanarius panamensis all preferred C. stercusmuscarum

shells. However, at the Garcia House, P. lepidus mainly

inhabited Morula, Tegula, and Turbo shells. Pylopagurus

roseus, a rare inhabitant at CEDO and the Garcia House,

chose Tegula and Turbo shells at both locations.

124   WRITING IN THE SCIENCES

TABLE I. Number of hermit crabs collected at Centro de Estudios de Desiertos y Oceanos and the Garcia House in Puerto Peñasco, Sonora, Mexico, on October 12-16, 1986.

	LOCATION	
HERMIT CRAB	CEDO	GARCIA HOUSE
Clibanarius digueti	461	54
Clibanarius panamensis	45	23
Dardanus sinistripes	0	9
Paguristes anahuacus	123	139
Pagurus lepidus	243	78
Pylopagurus roseus	11	7

tables placed on separate page, following the reference on page 6

TABLE II. Number of the most abundant snail shells (inhabited and empty) collected at Centro de Estudios de Desiertos y Oceanos and the Garcia House in Puerto Peñasco, Sonora, Mexico on October 12-16, 1986.

table's label and title placed above the illustration

	LOCATION	
SNAIL SHELL	CEDO	GARCIA HOUSE
Cerithium maculosum	140	22
Cerithium stercusmuscarum	1112	18
Columbella sp.	15	88
Morula sp.	189	340
Olivella sp.	49	14
Tegula sp.	48	168
Turbo sp.	44	355
Turitella sp.	24	2

Discussion

Upon first inspection, the results seem to indicate
that shell selection by hermit crabs is non-specific--the
crabs simply inhabit the most abundant snail shell in their
area. However, two of the five species of hermit crabs
collected did exhibit specific shell selection. Pylopagurus
roseus chose principally Tegula and Turbo shells at both CEDO
and the Garcia House, even though neither shell was common at
CEDO. Tegula and Turbo shells both have large percula,
therefore, it may be that P. roseus preferred these shells
because it has a large, flat, major chela that can act as an
operculum to seal the large opening against intruders.
Clibanarius panamensis also exhibited some shell selection.

There are several possible reasons why one species of
shell might be preferred over others. At CEDO, Morula and
C. maculosum shells were rarely inhabited, even though they
were the second and third most populous shells,
respectively. It may be that Morula shells were not chosen
because they are too small to protect the crab or they are
not heavy enough to stabilize the crab during tidal
currents.

Other investigators have also concluded that the
physical characteristics of a shell influence shell
selection by hermit crabs. The type of shell inhabited by a
crab is important because the shell size and shape can

*literature
survey
compares
findings
with existent
literature*

influence the crab's growth (2). Reese (8) found that
hermit crabs can discriminate between shells of different
snail species and between shells of different weights but of
the same species. A heavy shell may be more preferable
because it would prevent the crab from being washed away or
crushed by the surf (10). Blackstone observed that small
crabs have a strong preference for high-spired shells (2).
The shell also protects the hermit from predation by fish,
birds, brachyura crabs, and octopi (10), so a large shell
operculum would endanger the hermit. Vance (13) observed
that brachyurans mostly attacked hermits living in smaller
shells that leave more of the crab exposed and also that
hermits living in larger shells enjoyed greater protection.

A hermit crab may inhabit the most abundant snail
shell in a region because it actually prefers that shell
over other shells. If that particular shell is abundant in
an area, then its corresponding crab may also live in that
area. For instance, C. digueti was the most populous crab
at CEDO, but only the third most populous at the Garcia
House (Table III). The shell C. digueti inhabited at CEDO
was the most abundant but it was only the sixth most
abundant at the Garcia House. Thus, C. digueti was not
common there. Pagurus lepidus was the second most populous
crab at both locations, since one of its two favorite shells
was abundant at both places (Table III). Paguristes

*reference to
table in the
paper*

anahuacus was the most numerous hermit at the Garcia House,
but it was only the third most populous at CEDO; its three
preferred shells at the Garcia House were not common at CEDO.

TABLE III. Occurrence of hermit crabs in snail shells collected at *table within*
Centro de Estudios de Desiertos y Oceanos in Puerto Peñasco, *paper following*
discussion and
Sonora, Mexico, on October 12-16, 1986. *reference on*
page 9

SNAILS	CRABS				
	C. digueti	C. pana-mensis	P. ana-huacus	P. lepidus	P. roseus
C. maculosum	73	1	8	1	1
C. stercusmuscarum	357	30	98	165	0
Columbella sp.	0	0	0	2	0
Morula sp.	12	11	10	51	0
Olivella sp.	1	2	2	18	2
Tegula sp.	9	0	1	1	4
Turbo sp.	8	0	1	1	4
Turitella sp.	0	0	2	2	0
Acanthina angelica	0	1	1	0	0
Agaronia testacea	0	0	0	1	0
Eupleura muricifornes	0	0	0	1	0
Solenosteina capitanea	1	0	0	0	0
Total Crabs	461	45	123	243	11

conclusion

It is, therefore, the conclusion of the authors that shell selection by hermit crabs is a specific process. Although certain physical features (such as operculum size or weight) of the snail shell may explain why a certain shell is <u>not</u> selected, it is difficult to determine why a specific shell <u>is</u> selected.

Since our results indicate that environment affects snail shell distribution, which in turn affects hermit crab population (11), we advise that future work on hermit crab shell selection should include ecologically different collection sites. Environmental features such as current, predators, and habitat complexity affect the snail shell population and, thus, the hermit crab population (12). A physically diverse habitat increases the number of hermits in an area, because snails prefer to live in complex habitats. Therefore, shell selection studies conducted in the laboratory (8,4) may not produce accurate results, because environmental factors influence hermit crabs' choice of a specific shell in a particular region.

Acknowledgments

The authors wish to express their gratitude to Maggie Waldmann and Joyous Nicholopoulos for the use of their snail shell collections, which were invaluable in identification.

Literature Cited

1. Barth, R. H., and R. E. Broshears. 1982. The
   invertebrate world. Saunders College Publishing,
   Philadelphia, Pennsylvania.

2. Blackstone, N. W. 1985. The effects of shell size and
   shape on growth and form in the hermit crab Pagurs
   longicarpus. Biol. Bull. 168:75-90.

3. Brusca, R. C. 1980. Common intertidal invertebrates
   of the Gulf of California. The University of Arizona
   Press, Tucson, Arizona.

4. Grant, W. C., Jr. 1963. Notes on the ecology and
   behavior of the hermit crab, Pagurus acadianus.
   Ecol. 44:767-771.

5. Hazlett, B. A. 1967. Interspecific shell fighting
   between Pagurus bernhardus and Porgurus cuanensis
   (Decapoda, Paguridea) 29:215-220.

6. Hazlett, B. A. 1968. Effects of crowding on the
   agnostic behavior of the hermit crab, Pagurus
   bernhardus. Ecol. 49:573-575.

7. Mesce, K. A. 1982. Calcium-bearing objects elicit
   shell selection behavior in a hermit crab. Science
   215:993-995.

8. Reese, E. S. 1962. Shell selection behavior of hermit
   crabs. Anim. Behav. 10:337-360.

9. Reese, E. S. 1963. The behavioral mechanisms
   underlying shell selection by hermit crabs. Anim.
   Behav. 21:78-126.

10. Reese, E. S. 1969. Behavioral adaptations of
    intertidal hermit crabs. Amer. Zool. 9:343-355.

*capital letter
in first word
of title*

*title of journal
abbreviated*

*title of journal
not underlined*

130   WRITING IN THE SCIENCES

11. Spight, T. M. 1977. Availability and use of shells by intertidal hermit crabs. Biol. Bull. 152:120-133.

12. Vance, R. R. 1972a. Competition and mechanism of coexistence in three sympatric species of intertidal hermit crabs. Ecol. 53:1062-1074.

13. Vance, R. R. 1972b. The role of shell adequacy in behavioral interactions involving hermit crabs. Ecol. 53:1075-1083.

two works by the same author in the same year

SAMPLE SCIENCE PAPER—AUTHOR–DATE FORMAT

The Study of Fossil Flowers

by

Karen McCracken

Biology 241

Plant Systematics

Dr. Steven Seavey

Spring, 1984

McCracken 1

Abstract

The discovery of the earliest fossil angiosperm will be able
to tell paleobotanists much about the evolution of flowers.
The earliest accepted traces of angiosperms tell us that
they existed about 120 million years ago. As paleobotanists
pursue their search for fossil flowers, they encounter
technical difficulties as well as difficulties with the
current Linnean system of classification.

For hundreds of years, scientists have been fascinated
with the seemingly sudden rise and diversification of
angiosperms, or flowering plants, during the late Mesozoic
era. So far the earliest accepted traces of flowering plants
have been found about 120 million years ago in the Lower
Cretaceous period of the geologic time scale (see Appendix).
Before this time, it was the gymnosperms--plants that have no
true flowers, such as pines--that were abundant, but in
increasing numbers and complexity fossil angiosperms can be
found in later Cretaceous rocks. Most of the early
angiosperm record consists of pollen, seeds, fruits, and leaf
parts of the angiosperm. Fossil flowers are not as common
because the delicate structures were less likely to be
preserved. Still, paleobotanists continue to search for the
most ancient flower. This paper will look at the importance
of studying fossil flowers, what has been found, and what
difficulties have been encountered while studying fossil
flowers.

Fossil flowers can reveal extremely important
information about the time, place, and biological origin of
angiosperms. Also, fossil flowers are of particular interest
to paleobotanists since modern-day classification of
angiosperms is based primarily on floral morphology; seeds,
pollen, and leaf morphology are of only secondary importance.
With what we learn from each newly discovered fossil

flower we can test the many hypotheses about primitive

flowers that are made based on living angiosperms.

    Paleobotanists ultimately want to reveal the origin

of the angiosperm, but there are several questions

surrounding this general search for the origin of flowering

plants. First of all, paleobotanists wish to know where and

when angiosperms arose (Hughes 1976b). This can be answered

by where flowers are found in geologic strata and what other

types of fossils are found with them. Also of significance

to scientists is finding the family to which the primitive

flower belongs, or, in other words, which family of modern-

day angiosperms is the most primitive; recent literature

indicates that this is the most immediate question to be

resolved (Basinger and Dilcher 1984; Dilcher et al. 1976;

Friis and Skarby 1982; Hughes 1976b; Tiffney 1977). In

1915, Charles Bessey suggested that the most ancient flower

resembled flowers like the magnolias that are large,

bisexual, and insect pollinated, but others thought that the

first angiosperms were small, unisexual, and wind-pollinated

(Dilcher and Crane 1984). Although most botanists side

with Bessey, this debate has yet to be resolved by what can

be found in fossil flowers (Dilcher and Crane 1984). One

question that is raised by this argument is whether the

most primitive flowers were pollinated by insects or wind.

Since gymnosperms are primarily pollinated by wind and 85% of angiosperms are pollinated by insects, the answer could reveal information about the genetic lines along which angiosperms originated. Whether the first angiosperms were wind or insect pollinated can be answered by the morphology of fossil flowers. Another question pertaining to the evolution of angiosperms that could be resolved by further evidence is whether the flowering plants arose monophyletically or otherwise (Beck 1976). Finally, botanists are confronted with the difficulty of finding fossils to confirm their own speculations about the origin of angiosperms (Dilcher et al. 1976). To answer these many questions paleobotanists continue their search for the most primitive fossil flower.

In view of the fact that few fossil flowers have been found as yet, the ultimate goal to find enough evidence to explain the evolution of angiosperms seems unattainable. The most major fossil finds have been made in the past decade. Three various flower types are represented by mid-Cretaceous fossil flowers. The fossils have been dated as far back as Cenomanian age. Pollen and leaf fossils are the only evidence that angiosperms existed before this time. This evidence will be briefly discussed later. The diversity of the early fossil flowers appearing in the same age indicates that divergence occurred early in the history of angiosperms.

The most complete fossil flower was found in Nebraska
in the locality of Rose Creek (Basinger and Dilcher 1984;
Dilcher and Crane 1984). This flower is symmetrical with
five sepals and five petals. The sepals are joined at the
base and form a stiff shallow cup. The showy petals are
about half an inch long and spread out, alternating with the
sepals. There are also five stamens and five carpels. The
stamens have stout filaments and massive anthers which
spread out, lying against the petals. The pollen grains
found with these fossil flowers are extremely small (8 to 12
microns in diameter) with three sculpturing furrows.
Between the base of the stamens and carpels is a ring of
swollen tissue that is believed to have produced nectar,
indicating insect pollination. These fossil flowers are
most closely related to three living orders of angiosperms--
Saxifragales (Rosidae), Rosales (Rosidae), and Rhamnales
(Rosidae). Although similar to these orders, the fossil
flower could not be placed in any one of these orders since
none have the same floral features.

Another fossil flower, most like flowers of the order
Magnoliales, has been found in Kansas and is of similar age
to the previously described fossil flower (Dilcher and
Crane 1984). This is a large, solitary flower borne at the
end of a leafy shoot. The diameter of the flower is five to
six inches with three outer sepals and six to nine petals.

McCracken 6

The fossil shows scars where t he stamens were once
attached. There are believed to be 150 carpels which
each contain about 100 ovules, but only 20 to 40 developed
into seeds. Botanists believe that this flower was insect
pollinated because it was large and radially symmetrical.
The leaf structure suggests t hat this fossil flower belongs
to an extinct species because the leaf resembles no leaf of
any living angiosperm.

The third fossil flower is most widespread (Dilcher
and Crane 1984). Many small, apparently unisexual flowers
make up a spheroidal head about one-quarter of an inch in
diameter. About thirty-six heads are arranged in regular
intervals on a long axis. If there are any sepals or
petals, they are too small to be seen in the fossil. The
flowers have anywhere from four to seven carpels. Most
fossils show no sign of stamens; however, similar flowers
found in the USSR appear to have produced pollen. The
morphology suggests w ind pollination. This fossil flower
is most similar to th e genus Platanus or the sycamores.

Fossils of sec ondary structures such as stems and
leaves are more abu ndant than the flower parts since they
are more easily pr eserved in the geologic strata. The
earliest evidence indicating that angiosperms existed
before Cenomanian time are miospore fossils, which are
found in Berrias ian and Valanginian ages (Hughes 1976b).

These are fossils of spores or pollen of unknown function.
These miospore fossils provide no conclusive evidence of
the existence of angiosperms at the time. A small fruit,
Onoana californica, found in marine strata of Barremian age,
is one of the most important discoveries to paleobotanists
(Hughes 1976b). The genus was newly formed and placed in
the family Icacinaceae. This family is not regarded as
primitive but fossils of this family have been found in
Eocene deposits. A smaller species, O. nicanica, has also
been found in Aptian age strata in the USSR (Hughes 1976b).
Fossil leaves and woody structures have been found with
increasing abundance in later geological periods.

Paleobotanists confront several difficulties in their
search for the earliest angiosperms. One of the major
problems in solving the angiosperm mystery through fossil
flowers is the scarcity of the fossils themselves. The more
abundant, widely disseminated and robust the plant part,
the more likely it is to be preserved (Dilcher and Crane
1984). Because the cutin-covered surfaces of the secondary
structures (stems, leaves, seeds, and the walls of the
spores and pollen grain) are designed to keep water out,
these parts are more easily preserved than the reproductive
parts of the flower. Consequently the majority of the
fossil information is found in the secondary structures,
which reveal little information (Hughes 1976b). Fossils of

McCracken 8

early Cretaceous show only single organs or fragments and
the numbers increase steadily until whole plants can be
found in Turonian age (Hughes 1976a). Aside from the
difficulty in preservation, another explanation for the
lack of fossil flowers may be the location of origin of the
first angiosperm. If flowers first originated in upland
areas where there are no soil deposits, as opposed to
aggradational areas such as deltas, then the preservation
of flowers would be very rare.

Some general problems of data handling must be
resolved before many of the questions about angiosperm
origin can be answered. Most of the work with fossil
flowers goes directly into comparative morphology of living
angiosperms (Basinger and Dilcher 1984; Cronquist 1968;
Dilcher et al. 1976; Hughes 1976b). Although this is an
important aspect in the study of fossil flowers, the
tendency is often to overlook evolutionary elements. The
scientific belief that the "present is the key to the past"
allows botanists to assume many things about primitive
flowers and their evolution. This belief can lead to many
obstacles when parallels between extinct and living species
of angiosperms are drawn too closely (Hughes 1976a). The
current system for handling fossil data is the Linnean
system, which is the classification system used for modern-
day flowering plants. Norman Hughes (1976b) suggests that

this system is inadequate for paleontological material. He believes that a system needs to be designed where fossils can be conveniently analyzed and compared. Otherwise, as the system is now, retrieval is too difficult. Hughes' proposed paleontological system would provide time-correlation, geographic limits of the rock from which the specimen is taken, and the nomenclature for the specimen. This system could be helpful in comparison of fossils and would allow for easy data retrieval. Placing fossil flowers in the Linnean system forces botanists to find the family to which the fossil belongs. Often a fossil cannot be affiliated to one family because it is a representative of an extinct family. Another problem that hinders the study of fossil flowers is categorizing the actual structure of the flower as primitive or advanced. First of all, there may be differing views on what is primitive (Beck 1976). As mentioned earlier, most botanists believe a magnolia-type flower is most primitive but some also believe that a much smaller, unisexual flower is more primitive. For the most part, however, the analysis of a fossil flower as primitive or advanced has been helpful in separating fossil flowers from extant flowers (Hughes 1976b).

The fossil flowers have been useful in confirming most morphologists' belief of what is a primitive angiosperm (Dilcher et al. 1976), but still there are some

questions. Both insect and wind pollination existed in the
earliest fossil flowers, as seen earlier in the description
of the fossils. Further evidence of earlier ages needs to
be found to confirm which form of pollination is most
primitive. Fossils of later years can reveal much about the
coevolution of insects and flowers which brings up another
interesting area of study in fossil flowers (Crepet 1984).
Paleobotanists have been able to determine that angiosperms
first occurred at low latitudes in tropical areas. But the
most important question about the time of origin still
remains unanswered, although evolution must have taken place
before mid-Cretaceous as suggested by the diversity in the
fossils found in Cenomanian age and other fossil finds before
that age (Crepet 1984; Cronquist 1968; Dilcher et al. 1976;
Hughes 1976a). Finally, as far as the biological origin of
angiosperms is concerned, there is still much speculation.
Perhaps angiosperms have arisen from an undiscovered extinct
seed plant, or from gymnosperms, but little evidence supports
these hypotheses. Further study of the morphology of fossil
flowers can reveal more supporting evidence for these
speculations and new information for other hypotheses. By
continued concentration on the fossil record, in particular
fossil flowers, the mystery of the origin and evolution of
angiosperms can ultimately be resolved.

Appendix

Table showing sequence of ages of the Cretaceous period
(Hughes 1976b, fig. 7.1).

Era	Period	Age	Million years
Mesozoic	Cretaceous	Maestrichtian	65 ± 2
		Campanian	
		Santonian	
		Coniacian	
		Turonian	
		Cenomanian	(100)
		Albian	
		Aptian	
		Barremian	
		Hauterivian	
		Valanginian	
		Berriasian	135 ± 5

McCracken 12

References

Basinger, J. F., and D. L. Dilcher. 1984. Ancient bisexual flowers. Science 224:511-13.

Beck, C. B. 1976. Origin and early evolution of angiosperms: A perspective. In Origin and early evolution in angiosperms, ed. C.B. Beck, 1-10. New York: Columbia University Press.

Crepet, W. L. 1984. Ancient flowers for the faithful. Natural History, April, 39-44.

Cronquist, A. 1968. The evolution and classification of flowering plants. Riverside Studies in Biology. Boston: Houghton Mifflin Company.

Dilcher, D. L., and P. R. Crane. 1984. In pursuit of the first flower. Natural History, March, 57-60.

Dilcher, D. L., W. L. Crepet, C. D. Beeker, and H. C. Reynolds. 1976. Reproductive and vegetative morphology of a Cretaceous angiosperm. Science 191:854-56.

Friis, E. M., and A. Skarby. 1982. Scandianthus gen. nov., angiosperm flowers of saxifragalean affinity from the Upper Cretaceous of southern Sweden. Annals of Botany 50:569-583.

Hughes, N. F. 1976a. Cretaceous paleobotanic problems. In Origin and early evolution of angiosperms, ed. C.B. Beck, 11-22. New York: Columbia University Press.

————. 1976b. Palaeobiology of angiosperm origins: Problems of Mesozoic seed-plant evolution. Cambridge Earth Science Series. London: Cambridge University Press.

Tiffney, B. H. 1977. Dicotyledonous angiosperm flower from the Upper Cretaceous of Martha's Vineyard, Massachusetts. Nature 265:136-37.

Overview of Documentation Styles—Books

MLA Format (pp. 25–30)

Note in the text

> . . . Thoreau's reference to Abraham Lincoln (Miller 308).

Work listed at the end of the paper

> Miller, Perry. The American Transcendentalists: Their Prose
> and Poetry. New York: Doubleday, 1983.

Chicago Format (pp. 36–39)

Note in the text

> . . . acknowledged in 1902 with the Hay-Pauncefote
> Treaties.[1] . . .

Work listed at the end of the paper
Notes:

> 1. David Weigall, Britain and the World, 1815–1986 (New
> York: Oxford University Press, 1987), 107.

Bibliography:

> Weigall, David. Britain and the World, 1815–1986. New York:
> Oxford University Press, 1987.

APA Format (pp. 77–78)

Note in the text

> . . . a psychological profile of Adolph Hitler (Langer,
> 1972).

Work listed at the end of the paper

> Langer, W. C. (1972). The mind of Adolph Hitler. New York:
> Basic.

CBE Format (pp. 113–114)

Note in the text

. . . against a living snail has been documented (1, p. 432).

Work listed at the end of the paper

1. Barth, R. H. and R. E. Broshears. 1982. The invertebrate
    world. CBS College Publishing, Philadelphia,
    Pennsylvania.

Author-Date Format (See sample paper, pp. 131–143.)

Note in the text

. . . know where and when angiosperms arose (Hughes 1976b).

Work listed at the end of the paper

Hughes, N. F. 1976b. Palaeobiology of angiosperm origins:
    Problems of Mesozoic seed-plant evolution. Cambridge
    Earth Science Series. London: Cambridge University Press.

Overview of Documentation Styles—Articles

MLA Format (pp. 30–32)

> LeGuin, Ursula K. "American Science Fiction and the Other."
>
> Science Fiction Studies 2 (1975): 208–10.

Chicago Format (pp. 37–40)

Notes:

> 1. John Huntington, "Science Fiction and the Future,"
>
> College English 37 (Fall 1975): 340–58.

Bibliography:

> Huntington, John. "Science Fiction and the Future." College
>
> English 37 (Fall 1975): 340–58.

APA Format (pp. 78–80)

> Miller, W. (1969). Violent crimes in city gangs. Journal of
>
> Social Issues, 27, 581–593.

CBE Format (p. 114)

> 1. Cotton, F. A. Photooxidation and photosynthetic
>
> pigments. J. Cell. Biol. 87:32–43; 1987.

Author-Date Format (See sample paper, pp. 131–143.)

> Dilcher, D. L., W. L. Crepet, C. D. Beeker, and H. C.
>
> Reynolds. 1976. Reproductive and vegetative morphology
>
> of a Cretaceous angiosperm. Science 191:854–56.

INDEX